BIG GUY

BIG GUY
A School Horse Story

CELIA RYKER

Montpelier, VT

Big Guy ©2024 Celia Ryker

Release Date: June 18, 2024

All Rights Reserved.

Printed in the USA.

Published by Rootstock Publishing,
an imprint of Ziggy Media LLC
info@rootstockpublishing.com
www.rootstockpublishing.com

Softcover ISBN: 978-1-57869-173-9
Hardcover ISBN: 978-1-57869-174-6

Library of Congress Control Number: 2024906634

Cover and book design by Eddie Vincent, ENC Graphic Services.
Cover art and interior illustrations by Kathy Connell.

Author photo by Steven Nikola.

For permissions or to schedule a reading, contact the author at celia@celiaryker.com.

Dedicated to Fay
and lazy days
sitting on the pasture fence
wondering what the horses would sound like
if they could speak, and
guessing what they might say.

Contents

Big Guy's First School Horse Year

Chapter 1: A New Home 1
Chapter 2: My Earliest Memories. 4
Chapter 3: First Horse Show 8
Chapter 4: Madison Square Garden 14
Chapter 5: The Change 18
Chapter 6: Shorty 24
Chapter 7: Kicking 32
Chapter 8: The School Horse Pasture 36
Chapter 9: Long, Boring Stories 43
Chapter 10: The Life of a School Horse 47
Chapter 11: The Feed Room 53
Chapter 12: First Ride as a School Horse. 55
Chapter 13: Little Lisa 60
Chapter 14: My Herd 65
Chapter 15: Nancy Comes Back 71
Chapter 16: Brownie 74
Chapter 17: Switcheroo 80
Chapter 18: What's a Lion? 87
Chapter 19: Kaiser Is Back 91
Chapter 20: Circles 93
Chapter 21: Slippy Gets Caught 96
Chapter 22: The Dowsborough Woods 103
Chapter 23: Coyotes 106

Big Guy's Second School Horse Year

Chapter 24: The Zoo?!............................110
Chapter 25: Little Lisa's Lesson 113
Chapter 26: Kaiser's Trailer Arrives................117
Chapter 27: A New School Horse...................120
Chapter 28: Bucky's Big Escape 123
Chapter 29: Yellow Dog's Person...................131
Chapter 30: Missing Kaiser........................135
Chapter 31: The Stranger 139
Chapter 32: Is He All Right? 144
Chapter 33: Balloons..............................152
Chapter 34: Shorty's Sick 156
Chapter 35: A Real Horse.........................161

Glossary...164
Author's Note 167
Acknowledgments.................................168
About the Author 170
About the Artist 171

BIG GUY'S FIRST SCHOOL HORSE YEAR

Chapter 1

A New Home

"Sorry, old guy, but I think I'm taking you someplace you don't really want to go," said the man who snapped the lead rope to my halter and led me out of my stall. I wasn't sure what he meant, but I followed as always. Years of training left me little choice, but I was worried.

George doesn't know I can understand his words—humans rarely do. They don't realize horses communicate among themselves on a level similar to humans. Some humans know that when a horse lays its ears flat back it means trouble is coming. They can see and understand that, but they don't hear the messages that pass from horse to horse without sound or gesture.

George, my groom, is a gray-haired man who's worked with horses for most of his life. He feeds and waters us, grooms each horse with care, and cleans our stalls. George usually works alone, and he talks to us often.

"Move over one step, little lady, so I can clean out this back hoof here." He pats Taylor Maid's side and she moves over a step. George has twelve horses to care for and works with skilled efficiency.

This morning, though, his words were frightening. Where was he taking me that he didn't think I wanted to go? George left his hand on my neck as we walked into the school horse barn. We walked into a slip-stall, half the size of my usual stall. He snapped the rope attached to the feed rack to my halter and patted me again.

"Full Time, old man, I'm sorry to have to tell you this but you ain't a show horse no more, you're a school horse now. You'll be used for riding lessons. That's what school horses do; they're used to teach people how to ride. No more horse shows for you."

I knew what school horses were. They were in the barn next to the show barn. I could watch them out in the pasture from my private paddock. I had a small field to myself and they were turned out together in one big field. Sometimes I thought it would be fun to go outside with a group of horses, the way I had when I was very young. But show horses are different; our people value us too much to take a chance that we might hurt ourselves playing too hard. I used to walk past the school horses standing in their little stalls when I walked to the indoor arena.

Nibbling at the hay in front of me, I wondered how uncomfortable it would be to sleep in such a tiny stall. I could lie down and lean on the wall on either side, but I couldn't turn around or lie flat-out, the way I could in my old stall. I wondered if the other school horses had ever had the luxury of a box stall, like I'd had. They may not know what they're missing—but I did.

My skinny new stall had a window with a view of the

parking lot, but I didn't see what I was looking at; my mind was replaying the events that led me here.

Chapter 2

My Earliest Memories

My earliest memories are filled with nursing, learning to graze, and playing with other youngsters in a rolling green field that went on forever. My mother's chestnut coat was my anchor. No matter where I ran or how fast I moved, I could spot her coppery coat a mile away.

I asked her one day, "Why am I bay and you're chestnut?"

My coat was a deep brown and my mane and tail were black. Cliff, the groom who'd helped fill out my registration papers, had called out "bay" to the woman filling out the paperwork. She'd looked at her clipboard and said, "Let's start from the top. What's his registered name?"

"Full Time, thoroughbred, colt . . ."

"Not so fast, give me time to write this down." I had never seen this woman. She stared at her papers as she asked, "What white markings are on his face?"

"Star and snip."

She looked up from her papers. I had a white mark in

the center of my forehead and a little strip of white on my muzzle. As she wrote, the woman said, "Four white socks." I never saw the writing woman again, but when she left I knew I was a bay thoroughbred colt with a star, a snip, and four white socks. Cliff, the first groom in my life, had been calling me Full Time, so I knew my name.

My mother's name was Copper Harbor and she was the color of a penny. Her mane and tail were almost the same color as her coat, and she told me that made her a chestnut. Most of the horses in the field had white markings on their faces or legs, but Copper Harbor had not one white hair.

Almost all of my pasture-mates were the same or nearly the same color as their mothers, and I had been wondering about this. But it wasn't until Brownie commented about my dark coloring compared to my mother's red coat that I thought to ask her.

Brownie was a pushy little pony who'd been in the field since my first day outside. He was almost the same size as me, but he was three years old and I was still a baby. He said his full name was Our Dear Precious Little Brownie, but he didn't seem little or precious to the foals he bossed around.

Mother nuzzled my shoulders as she answered my questions. It felt so good to be rubbed there, my knees began to buckle and I almost didn't hear her. "Your father was a racehorse, related to Man o' War—that's a big deal. He was tall and dark, like you, with a wide white blaze down his face and four white legs. You look a lot like him."

"What was his name?" I had never heard about my father.

Copper Harbor shook her head and neck. "I don't know if I ever heard his name. We only met once and he talked so much about Man o' War, it didn't dawn on him to tell me his own name."

She stopped nuzzling me and stood back a step, gazing across the pasture, and said, "He certainly was handsome. You're going to be every bit as handsome, but don't let it go to your head, sweet boy."

Brownie was with me when I was weaned. The foals in our herd were all about six months old when we were separated from our mothers. The mares were led to a trailer; our moms called to us, but their voices were muted when the trailer door closed, and they faded as the trailer drove away.

We were frantic, running in circles and calling out for our mothers. I wondered where my mother was going and when she would be back. I didn't know if I would ever see her again.

On weaning day, Brownie grazed and wandered as if nothing was wrong. After a while the foals did the same. We followed him wherever he went, the way we had followed our mothers.

Brownie kept telling us that it was time to grow up. "You're not babies anymore—get used to it."

He wasn't friendly but he was with us as he always had been, the center of our herd, until we went off to be trained. I didn't realize how much growing up I had ahead of me.

Chapter 3

First Horse Show

I was nearly three years old and had been in training for months when I heard Jim, my trainer, talk about preparing me for my first horse show. I didn't know what that meant but I felt an excitement in the barn. It was clear that something big was coming.

I was groomed often and had learned to stand quietly in the cross ties. A chain was attached to both sides of my halter and secured to the walls on either side of me whenever I was groomed.

My grooming sessions were becoming longer, and more intense, as the horse show approached. Cliff, my groom, combed through my mane as usual, then wrapped a few strands around the comb and pulled them out of my neck. *Ouch. What is this new grooming method?*

"Sorry, buddy, but you're going to your first horse show next week and you need to be neat and tidy." He pulled a few more hairs out. "This makes your mane shorter and easier to braid. You have to be braided for the hunter shows. I'm not sure why, but that's the way it goes."

When he was done my whole neck was a little tingly—not quite painful but not good either. When my muzzle and ears had been shaved, Cliff put the clippers away and plucked the few long hairs that stuck out above and below my eyes.

"Gotta get rid of these guard hairs—we want your face to be perfection in the show ring." It didn't hurt much, and I loved it when Cliff stood back and looked me over. "You just went from good-looking to handsome. Your conformation is nearly perfect, you're a great mover, you jump like a gazelle, and now you have the best-looking face in the barn. You should be something else in the show ring."

I strutted back to my stall.

Jim rode me in my first horse show. It was scary—in a new place with new jumps. I was accustomed to Jim's arena. There were a few more shows that summer, then we trained indoors through the winter months to be ready to show again in the spring. My second summer on the show circuit was fun. I realized that I was good at this, and I loved the praise I got from Jim.

I heard him talking to other people at the show: "This guy has great potential—he's won almost every class I've entered him in."

I didn't realize I was for sale until a potential buyer took me home on trial. His name was Daniel, and I didn't understand him. Jim sat lightly on my back, his signals smooth and subtle. Daniel bobbled around—sometimes I thought he might fall off. When I didn't understand what he wanted, he became harsh—tugging, jabbing, kicking. Jim had never done that, and I was confused during every ride. I dreaded seeing Daniel walking toward my stall with his saddle.

"He's just not working out." Daniel led me toward the trailer where Jim was waiting. I was glad to get back in Jim's trailer. I wanted to tell him it was Daniel who wasn't working out.

Back at Jim's farm, everything fell back into place. I was with my old stable-mates, and we traveled to horse shows almost every weekend. I was ridden by many potential buyers—none as difficult as Daniel, but there were a couple I hoped never to see again.

Nancy's first ride was tentative; she was nervous. She didn't make any big mistakes but her tension made me uncomfortable. She returned the next day, less nervous, and after the ride she asked, "Can I walk him out in the field?"

"You're the biggest, prettiest horse I have ever seen." She patted my neck. "My father says that you're too big for me. I'm only twelve, but I'm tall for my age. I'm going to see if he'll bring me back one more time before he makes up his mind. I know your name is Full Time but if you were my horse I would only use that name for horse shows. I would call you Big Guy."

Nancy became my person and I loved my nickname. I was her Big Guy.

She took me to shows the way Jim had, and I took pride in winning more than the other horses from our farm. Taylor Maid, who's nickname was TM, got mad when I rubbed it in if she got third in the same class I won. I remembered my mother saying "don't let your good looks go to your head," but she didn't know how talented I would be. After Taylor Maid's angry words I knew to keep my talent to myself. I couldn't help it if I was a great mover, great jumper, good looking, and won all the time.

Between the shows, back on the farm, we were kept in our stalls most of the day. We were turned out in a paddock to run and play for an hour or two, and exercised for about the same length of time almost every day. I got to know Taylor Maid and Ding, who were stabled on either side of me. Painted Doll's stall was across the aisle from mine. We were never turned out together because our people were afraid we might hurt ourselves if we played too hard, but we became friends anyway.

I was surprised when I came in from my paddock one day and found an animal sleeping in my feed tub. I sniffed at it but it didn't move much, just curled up and went back to sleep.

"There's a little animal in my feed tub," I said out loud.

"That's the new kitten. She was sleeping in my feed tub yesterday," Ding said. "Just push her out of the way with your nose, but be careful—she might scratch. I've dealt with barn cats before."

I pushed her with my nose, but

she curled her soft paws around my muzzle and made a funny noise. "She's making weird noises."

"That's purring," Taylor Maid said. "That means she likes you. I like having barn cats around, especially when they purr."

George, our groom, called the kitten Lady Bug. I often found her sleeping in my feed tub. Sometimes when George poured the grain in, it piled on top of her. Then she would move so I could eat.

On cold winter nights she slept near me. Sometimes she would curl up on my back, and other times she pushed herself against my chest and lay in the bedding next to me.

She slept with other horses sometimes, and I missed her. Over the years I met other barn cats at home and horse shows, but Lady Bug was special.

Chapter 4

MADISON SQUARE GARDEN

The first time I went to Madison Square Garden for the National Finals—the most important horse show of the year—I knew it was a big deal. Nancy had been increasingly nervous as the show approached. I had been in cities before. I could feel how far away the nearest open space was, and it made me uncomfortable.

We drove to New York City in the biggest van I had ever been in. We traveled with strange horses and were handled by grooms we had never seen before. Everything was a little off-kilter, and when I stepped off the van I had no sense of where the nearest open space might be. I had never been in a city this big before.

Ding was so rattled that, when a car door slammed he jumped back, pulled away from his handler, and took off. I saw his legs, wrapped in shipping bandages, running into a street full of cars next to a sidewalk full of people, his lead shank fluttering behind him. Taylor Maid looked like she wanted to follow Ding, but we were rushed away onto a broad ramp that went up and up and up. *Where were we going? What's going to happen to Ding?* We were getting further and further from the ground, and I didn't like it. We had to move close to the wall twice to let a truck go by in the opposite direction. The ramp was solid and wide like a road, but it didn't feel like any road I had ever been on.

Nancy was waiting for me, standing on what looked like dirt—but it didn't feel right. "Here you are." She took my lead rope and led me to a large, well-bedded stall. "Isn't this wild, Big Guy? The ground floor of the stadium is five flights up but you can't feel it at all."

Maybe she couldn't feel it, but I was too far from the ground. I've never been in a tree but I imagined this was what birds must feel like, up so high in the branches, the ground far away.

Taylor Maid and I had hay to eat, but we were uncomfortable up in the air and worried about Ding until we saw him being led down our barn aisle. I call it a barn aisle but the ceiling was too high and the ground vibrated under the bedding. Do branches vibrate under the birds? A groom I didn't recognize put Ding in the stall between Taylor Maid and me, and patted him on the neck. "Now, let's not go running down Seventh Avenue again, mister."

"What happened?" I asked.

"I got scared," Ding said. "I thought I could get away. This is the weirdest place I've ever been."

Nancy was running a brush over me; I couldn't tell what time it was. The lights had been on all night, but I knew it wasn't morning yet.

"Our designated time to get into the main arena to practice is four a.m." Nancy wasn't talking to me—she'd been talking to herself a lot since we'd gotten to New York.

"I hope you're ready, Big Guy. We have one hour and I don't know how many people will be out there with us." I'm more relaxed when she talks to me.

The arena was huge and voices echoed in the empty stadium. Taylor Maid whinnied from her stall, and I answered.

"You two have never done that before."

Talk to me, Nancy, I've never been this nervous.

Once we started to work, we both settled down. Walk, trot, canter, warm-up over a cross pole. This is the first normal moment since we got off the van. The fences were big and pretty, and easy to jump.

"We can do this." Nancy felt better too.

We adapted to our treehouse stable and did our best at that show, but our riders were nervous in ways we had never experienced; even Ben, the riders' coach, was anxious. I hardly recognized Nancy when we entered the show ring, she'd forgotten how to ride since the morning warm-up. *Talk to me, Nancy.*

In our second class she patted my neck as we entered the ring. "We didn't crash and burn in that first class—let's try to do even better this time, Big Guy." We both perform better when she talks to me.

The warm-up area was small and crowded, and I wasn't

sure where to go. The practice fences only allowed a few strides off a tight corner. Turn, jump, land, turn. The announcer was so loud and there were people and horses everywhere.

We didn't win a single ribbon at that show; that had never happened to me. The following year at the same show, Nancy and I won second-, fourth-, and sixth-place ribbons. We went back for two more years—Nancy almost lost her mind when we won first place in an equitation class. Madison Square Garden was exciting but exhausting. We were all glad to relax and get time off after that show.

Chapter 5

THE CHANGE

Receiving ribbons and trophies had become my life. I loved to jump, but the flat classes were boring and too easy. We walked, trotted, and cantered in a circle around the judge. It didn't make much sense to me, but we often worked in circles to warm up before jumping. Nancy said I moved like a grass trimmer, my stride long and close to the ground. My toes brushed along the blades of grass when I trotted. I guess that's one of the reasons I won so many of my under-saddle classes—I got ribbons for doing almost nothing.

Jumping over fences was more fun. I could pull my knees up so high, and I loved the classes that required jumping bigger fences. The little jumps were a waste of my time and talent. Nancy got excited when we did well, and she always patted my neck and cooed to me as we left the arena.

"Big Guy, you're the best."

After the last class of the day she would give me a minty

hard candy as a reward. I could taste it when I heard the rustle of the candy wrapper. She told me many times how much she loved me and how great I was. Sometimes I thought about my mother, who'd told me not to get cocky about my good looks. For years I brought home more ribbons than any other horse in the barn.

Whack! The day I hit a rail and felt the sting on my front legs hurt my pride as well as my shins. I was losing the spring that I used to feel. My joints ached at the end of a show day. Some days I hurt a little all day long.

What's going to happen if I can't jump this high anymore? What will Nancy do with me if I don't win ribbons?

Medication helped. I didn't like the taste of it, and it upset my stomach a little, but with it I could jump like I used to and it was worth the tummy grumble to feel so good in the air. But we still weren't winning as much. I was accustomed to winning blue ribbons—seconds and thirds were a giant step down. I heard conversations about arthritis and age. Nancy cried sometimes.

"I love you, Big Guy." Her hand held a sweet treat that I didn't deserve.

Nancy was seventeen years old when she knelt next to me

and wrapped my legs the way she had on every show day, but why was she crying this time? We'd won two classes and were second in another. I was having a bad day yesterday, but things went well today. *Why is she so upset? Here comes her father, he'll make her feel better.*

"Nancy, I'm sorry you heard that."

"Sorry I heard it, or sorry that the medication that works best on Full Time's arthritis will destroy his stomach? I don't want blue ribbons that badly."

"We just did it to get to the end of the show season," he said

"You would risk his life for a few more shows?"

"You're not being fair. The vet said it *can* cause stomach ulcers, not that it *will* cause them."

"Why didn't you tell me that?" Nancy stood up, wiping her hands on her pant leg.

"I didn't know," he said.

"Now that we know, what should we do?" Nancy put the cap on the liniment bottle.

"We may have to sell Full Time and buy you a new horse."

They're talking about me. They're going to replace me?

Nancy patted my neck. "We can't do that. What if the new owner decides to use the meds to get every last show they can from him? I couldn't take that chance." Her warm hand rested on my neck

"Nancy, I can't afford to board two horses," her father said. All my stable mates were owned by different people. I was glad Nancy was my person, but now I wasn't so sure about her father's words.

They only need one horse. I'm right here, and I showed well today.

"Then I'll give this up and stop showing." She scratched behind my left ear and I tipped my head.

"You don't mean that," he said.

"Dad, you've known me all my life. I have a year left to show as a junior. I would like to show amateur when I age out, but I would give that up for him." She scratched under my jaw, and my upper lip twisted.

"We don't have to make this decision now," he said. "We can talk to your mom tonight and see if she has any ideas."

The cellophane crinkled and I took the red-and-white ball of hard candy from Nancy's hand.

That night, Painted Doll asked from the next stall, "Are you all right?"

"I feel fine now, but I hurt all over yesterday."

"Yeah, I've heard about that with other horses, and then they just disappear. I've often wondered where they went."

Taylor Maid spoke from her stall. "They get sold. That happens sometimes whether you're young or old."

Painted Doll replied, "I wasn't asking about how you felt physically, Big Guy, but how you felt about being sold again. The change is always difficult, even if you go to a good home. I was so worried when I first got here. I had one potential buyer who took me home for two weeks and then returned me to the seller because *I didn't work out*. I didn't work out because that little girl couldn't ride."

"You don't need to worry about me," I said. "I don't think Nancy will sell me."

"Oh, Big Guy, junior riders don't get to make that decision—their parents do," Taylor Maid said.

"Thanks, Taylor Maid, I feel much better now." I picked at my hay and wondered what might happen. The sweet alfalfa was tasteless.

On my last morning as a show horse, the blacksmith arrived to pull my shoes for my post-show season rest period. At the end of each show season I spent a few weeks resting, and they left me barefoot for that. He pulled my rear shoes and trimmed my hooves. That was odd, he usually started with my front feet. Then he pulled my front shoes and trimmed the hooves, but when I thought he was finished he nailed on new front shoes. They were heavier than my usual shoes. Were they trying to make me stronger by making me wear a heavier shoe? I had struggled at the end of this year's show season, but I was sure a brief rest would set things straight.

I clip—thump-clop—thumped out of the barn and up the gradual slope to the upper barn. I was accustomed to the clip—clop-clip—clop of shod hooves or the thump—thump-thump—thump of bare feet; this morning, my steps sounded foreign to me.

I had walked through the upper barn many times on my

way to the indoor arena for my exercise regimen, past the rumps of the ten school horses that lived there. They stood in slip-stalls, not roomy boxes, and every third stall had a window. In the lower barn the stalls were twelve-by-twelve foot squares and each one had its own window. In the slip stalls, the horses could stand and lay down, but they couldn't turn around. They were tied in place by a rope attaching their halter to the feed rack in the front of the stall and a chain draped behind them to keep them from backing into the aisle. The school horses ate their grain and hay from the flat wooden rack they were tied to.

My box stall had room for me to walk around, and I could lie flat on my side if I wanted to. In my youth I'd taken pride in standing most of the time. I could sleep standing up, but, as I got older, I preferred to lie down to sleep. Lately, though, I found myself lying down in the middle of the day.

Usually when I walked past the school horses I would be on my way to the indoor arena, wearing my saddle and bridle. Today I wore only my halter. Was George going to turn me out in the arena? He does that when the turn-out paddocks are icy, but the weather is perfect today—maybe I'll be lounged in the arena. I didn't understand why, but there were days when I wasn't ridden but tethered on a long line walking, trotting, and cantering in a circle around Nancy for no apparent reason. But she wasn't here today. I was alone. I was a school horse now.

Chapter 6

Shorty

My First Day in the School Horse Barn

"Are you all right?" The words came from the stall on my left. Through the gaps between the two-by-twelve-inch oak boards between us, a small chestnut mare spoke to me. "My name is Shorty."

I shook my head, then did a full-body shake. "I was just thinking."

"I don't recommend doing too much of that." These words came from the stall on my right, where a dark brown, almost black, gelding stood.

On my left, Shorty lifted her head so I could see her right eye. "His name is Kaiser," Shorty said. "He doesn't have what you would call a sunny disposition."

"Her name is Short Stuff." Kaiser sneered.

"Well," Shorty said, "Kaiser's full name is *I Was Kaiser*

Bill's Batman, and he hates it. So if he starts to get on your nerves, use his registered name. It gets him every time. Kaiser, can you be pleasant to our new arrival?"

"I'll give it a try, Queen Shorty. So, new guy, what's your name?"

"Full Time."

"Is that your registered name? Do you have a short name?" Kaiser was certainly curious.

"My registered name is Full Time."

I struggled to think of a shortened name but the only thing I could think of was how Nancy called me Big Guy, but that's no shorter than Full Time.

"Come on, Big Guy, we're in the next class," Nancy said as she ran a brush over my already gleaming coat and set my saddle in place. "This is an equitation class. They're judging the way I ride, how I sit, how smoothly I get you to walk, trot, and canter. I don't usually do much in the equitation division, but today may be the day."

Nancy had told me about her frustration with the equitation classes. She spoke as if she knew I could understand her, but I was pretty sure she didn't think I comprehended a word. Sometimes her eyes misted as she spoke. I felt bad for her, but didn't know what I could do. She felt comfortable and smooth on my back. *What were the judges looking for?*

Two weeks before, I'd heard Nancy talking about a

problem she called scoliosis. "My trainer thinks it may be the reason for my equitation problem," she had said.

Nancy's spine wasn't as straight as it should be. She told me that once, but I'd known it the first time she sat on my back. She was excited as she spoke. "My trainer, who's been teaching me since I was nine years old, said he'd noticed one of my shoulder blades showing up against my hunt coat while the other looks like it isn't there. This makes it look like I'm twisting my body when I'm actually sitting straight, and the judges mark me down for it," she said.

"My grandmother's going to make a fake left shoulder blade and sew it into my hunt coat. My new jacket will make it look like both shoulder blades are the same."

The first time she wore her new jacket into the show ring she patted my neck and said, "This is the test, Big Guy. Today I find out if my shoulder blade falsie works."

We rode our course of fences as usual, and nothing had changed—she felt the same as she always had on my back. I was disappointed for Nancy, she had been so excited about improving her placing. The last horse completed the course, and when the results were announced Nancy's name was called first. She squealed and clambered into the saddle to trot into the ring for her first equitation blue ribbon. She fed me a piece of minty hard candy as she led me back to the barn. "Well, Big Guy, the shoulder falsie is here to stay."

"Nancy calls me Big Guy."

"Well that's an appropriate name—what are you, seventeen hands?" Kaiser isn't much taller than Shorty, who is fifteen hands. At only two inches taller than a pony, she's awfully short for a horse. I might ask her about that sometime, but not today. She might be sensitive about her height.

Some shows had a division for smaller horses, but I always went into the taller group. "I'm 17.1," I tell them.

As we talked, we munched hay from the flat table before me, where we would be served both hay and grain. There was a water bucket in the corner, hanging from a hook. It was like the bucket in my old stall, and the water was clear and fresh. The stall was small but clean and comfy. Shorty was explaining the school-horse schedule to me.

"Almost all lessons are in the afternoon and evening hours, so people can come after school and work. On Saturday and Sunday we're busy all day long. Jane tries to keep us from working more than two hours in one day, but sometimes on the weekend the popular horses might get an extra hour."

"The popular horses," Kaiser said in a sarcastic tone as he kicked at the wall between us. "Every little kid wants to ride Shorty because she's short and cute, and she puts her head down so they can hug her. I don't know why she does that; it means more work for her."

"Oh, Kaiser, you have your fans." Shorty sounded like my mother, sweet and kind. "Once they start jumping over bigger fences, many students want to ride you. You jump better than I do."

"Yeah, yeah." Kaiser let me see his left eye between the boards. "Don't let them hug your head, Big Guy, or you'll never get a moment's rest."

"Kaiser, stop talking like that. Big Guy hasn't even had the chance to look around yet."

I thought it was funny that Shorty thought I would take more than a few minutes to inspect my new stall. The barn is smaller than the boarder barn, but I think it has as many horses in it, maybe more. I can hear munching, scuffling, and bumping all around me.

"I should introduce you to everyone. Would you like that?" Shorty was being so polite, I had to say yes.

"You've already met Kaiser. The next horse after me is Smokey."

I could see that he was small and gray but not much more than that. Golden Boy was in the next stall, and I couldn't see him at all.

Shorty said, "He's an ex-racehorse. I thought he was tall until I met you."

Golden Boy said, "He may be taller but I'll bet I'm faster. I beat some pretty tall horses in my day."

Kaiser butted in, "Your day was long ago and far away."

Shorty continued her introductions. "In the next stall is Tom Jones."

I was thinking that was an odd name when Kaiser explained, "His person, Ben, said he gave him that name because of his Roman nose."

From three stalls away Tom Jones added, "I got the name because, like Tom Jones the singer, I have talent. I can jump a darn site better than you, Mr. Batman."

"Children, children, please behave. I have more introductions to make." Shorty sounded like my mother correcting the young foals. I wanted to be nice to her, but I didn't think I could remember all these names. I couldn't see most of the horses that went with them.

"Across the aisle, behind you, is Star Shadow."

I could see a lean, dappled-bay rump, but nothing more.

The stall directly behind me held a yellow, solidly muscled rump that looked like it belonged to a quarter horse. Shorty saw me looking at him. "That's Yellow Dog," she said.

Over my left shoulder, the next stall was filled up with a horse that looked like he could pull a wagon.

"That's Slippy, he's part Clydesdale."

Kaiser chimed in, "Slippy's real name is Slivovitz, after some crude Hungarian whisky."

"It's a plum brandy, if you don't mind." Slippy's voice sounded as solid as his haunches looked.

Shorty politely continued to introduce the next horse, Nugget, another palomino quarter horse, more golden than Yellow Dog, who was definitely yellow.

I could barely see the next horse, Paper Moon, who seemed lean and gray, almost white. The last horse was Noble Road, and I couldn't see him at all.

"He's named after the road the farm was on where they picked him up. How original is that?" Kaiser invited Noble Road's response.

"It's better than being named after some weird whistling song called *I Was Kaiser Bill's Batman*, whatever that means," called out Noble Road.

I wondered why Kaiser made fun of other horse's names when he didn't like his own, so I asked, "Why don't you like your name, Kaiser? Don't you like the song?"

"It's a whistling song—hearing a short whistle is not bad but listening to a human whistle and whistle and whistle is awful." Kaiser shook his head and neck. "I get a headache just thinking about it. The guy who gave me that name whistled that song all the time. I threw him to the ground one day just to make him stop," he said.

"That was a mistake," he continued. "He made me his training project and rode me even more. I behaved, but I hated that song. I haven't heard it in years, and I'm glad."

Shorty added, "There's a pony in the little stall beyond the feed room. You can meet him tomorrow."

I had to tell her, "Shorty, I'll never remember all these names."

"Don't worry, you'll meet them all tomorrow morning when we get turned out together."

I hadn't thought about the fact that I would be outside with all these horses. I hadn't been out with another horse since I was two years old. I wasn't sure how I felt about that.

"In the summer we stay out all night." Kaiser sounded like that was a good thing.

The barn was fairly quiet. The farm was officially closed on Mondays. A wheelbarrow was being wheeled down the aisle behind me, and two flakes of hay were thrown over my head, hit the wall in front of me, and dropped to the wooden feed deck. A groom I didn't recognize brought in my scoop of sweet feed and poured it on top of the hay. The school horses received the same grain as the show horses; a sweet mixture of oats and corn with a hint of bran, coated with a touch of sweet molasses.

The munching of grain and hay had almost stopped,

quieting the barn once more and the lights were off, when Kaiser started kicking.

Chapter 7

Kicking

Thud! Thud! Thud! Thud! Thud! The first thud surprised me. By the fifth I asked Shorty, "What's he doing?"

"Kicking the wall. He says it fills the boredom, but I think he just likes to kick. If your rider steers you too close to him during a lesson, he'll threaten to kick at you. If you don't move away fast enough, he will."

"He would kick me for just getting near him?" I had stopped counting the number of blasts that shook the wall on the far side of Kaiser's stall.

"He usually misses, and when he does connect it's not much of a hit—but don't tell him that. I think he might kick harder if you thought he wasn't strong enough or fast enough to hurt you." Shorty was finishing up her hay. She ate slower than most horses.

"Does he do this all night?"

"No—" Shorty was interrupted by a crashing sound

beyond the wall Kaiser was kicking. "He doesn't kick during the day because Jane or someone else will shout at him and maybe give him a swat to make him stop. But when the barn closes down for the night, he starts to kick."

There was another crashing sound beyond Kaiser's stall, and Shorty laughed. "Two down, four to go." Another crash, and she corrected, "Three to go."

"What's falling in there?" I asked.

"Saddles. That's the tack room where our saddles and bridles are kept." There was another crash. "Two to go. There are usually six saddles on the racks beyond that wall, and Kaiser doesn't stop kicking until he's knocked them all to the floor."

"How do you know what's in there?"

Shorty nuzzled around for the last of her hay. "Kaiser dragged one of his young riders in there when he was being led back to his stall after a lesson. He saw the door open and turned his head to drag the little girl through the door with him. He said it's full of saddle racks and bridles hanging everywhere."

Kaiser stopped kicking for a moment. "I pooped in there too." His kicking resumed and two more thuds followed.

I noted, "Those two sounded different."

"They're on the bottom racks. The top saddles have farther to fall, so they make more noise. Now we might be able to get some rest." Shorty searched the floor under the hay shelf for any morsels she might have missed.

"Those bottom two saddles are harder to get. It takes a stronger kick to knock them down." Kaiser was proud of himself.

Shorty eased herself to the floor of her stall, leaning on the wall between us. "Nightie-night, all."

I lay down leaning on the same wall. I could feel the tips of Shorty's long coat barely touching mine. I fell asleep comforted by her slow, easy breathing.

Alone in my paddock, I used to watch the school horses charge out of the barn and mill around in the big open field. If I was turned out later in the day I would hear a whistle and the school horses would run back to the gate to go back into the barn.

Sometimes, when I watched the schoolies, as we called them, wandering their huge pasture, I felt nostalgic for the days when I did that with my young friends. But then I remembered they were school horses and I was a show horse. Their coats were never as shiny and well-kept as mine and all the other horses on the show string.

The school horses grew long winter coats, but I hadn't had a real winter coat in years. I was blanketed and kept under lights for a prescribed time each day, so my body wouldn't want to grow a long coat. The lights fooled my body into thinking it was summer. I once watched a horse come in from Canada who had a long winter coat, but after a couple of weeks under the lights he began to shed down to his summer coat.

As a school horse I'm going to have a shaggy winter coat

and I'll listen to Kaiser kick saddles down every night. I miss my big stall and show horse friends.

Chapter 8

THE SCHOOL HORSE PASTURE

Jane pushed a wheelbarrow heaped with sweet feed down the aisle behind our stalls, delivering our breakfast. Each horse got one scoop. She ducked under the chain behind me and ran her hand along my left side as she walked to the front of the stall and poured the grain in the corner of the wooden deck in front of me. In the corner I could clean up every bit of grain without chasing it around the wooden deck.

"Here you go Big Guy, your first breakfast in your new home. I know your name is Full Time but Nancy told me that she called you Big Guy and I think it suits you." The sound of munching filled the barn, much as it had in the boarder barn. I was accustomed to getting hay with my morning grain but no hay was provided.

I wondered what it was going to be like out in a big field with all of these horses.

Since show horses are valuable and people didn't want to

risk us harming one another, our time in the paddock was always spent alone. When turned out alone in my paddock, I wore protective leather boots that shielded and supported my legs from ankle to knee—the part of my leg that felt the most strain when landing after a jump—so that I wouldn't get hurt if I played too hard outside.

I'm about to go into a pasture with all of these horses, and I won't have boots or leg wraps. What if Kaiser kicks me? What if they chase me around until I hurt myself? I thought of one "what if?" after another.

"This is going to be a little confusing at first, Big Guy, so I'll guide you through the program." Jane backed me out of the stall, then turned us around and unhooked the chain behind Kaiser's stall. He began to back out immediately, and I worried he might try to kick me. But he walked down the aisle toward the door. Jane had already freed all the horses from the ropes tying them to their feed racks, so they were ready to leave their stalls when she unhooked the rump chains. Star Shadow had turned around in her stall and walked down the aisle after Kaiser. Jane unhooked all the rump chains for Shorty, Slippy, Nugget, Smokey, Golden Boy, Paper Moon, Tom Jones, and Noble Road. I couldn't believe I remembered all their names. The last horses were cantering to catch up with horses that were already out of sight around the corner.

Jane turned around and we went back into the barn, past the empty stalls, the tack room on the left, and another closed door on the right, to a miniature slip stall in the corner. I had never seen a stall that small. Jane unhooked the rear chain and a pony backed out. The pony was dun-colored, somewhere between brown and yellow, like the butterscotch hard candies Nancy sometimes fed me when she ran out of the mints. The pony had a dark dorsal stripe from his mane to his tail. He turned toward the far door and began to canter.

"That's Brownie." I couldn't believe my eyes. *That's Our-Dear-Precious-Little-Brownie! I know that pony. I knew that pony when I was a foal. I know him!*

I found myself bouncing up and down, trotting in place next to Jane. She gave my lead rope a couple of jerks. "Steady there, Big Guy, you'll get your turn."

I bounced beside Jane toward the door, and when we stepped outside and turned left I saw the gate open to a vast pasture. All the horses were out there, but I was only interested in Brownie, Dear-Precious-Brownie, and I bounced a little higher.

"Steady now." Jane snapped the rope again.

We went through the gate, turned around, and Jane pulled the gate shut and latched it before unsnapping my lead rope, and I bolted off to find my old friend.

Three strides into the field I was surrounded; all the schoolies were pushing and sniffing and talking. Shorty was the first to step out from the crowd. She was rounder than she had looked through the gap between the boards in our stalls. All the other horses pushed in so close, I couldn't see much of anything.

I couldn't move in the crowd. The noise and pushing was worse than any of the "what ifs?" I had imagined. I thought I was going to be crushed, stepped on, or kicked, but I didn't have enough space to fight back. Eventually the group eased back and the noise settled, but not by much. I wasn't going to be crushed, but I still couldn't get away.

Slippy's broad bay head was the second one I recognized in the mob. Its size matched the huge haunches I had seen last night. His wide white blaze was blocked off by a thick black forelock that hung halfway down his face. His overgrown mane fell in a mat on both sides of his neck and looked like it had never been properly cared for.

"I'm Golden Boy." A lean red chestnut pushed his way in front of me before I could say a word to Slippy. Golden Boy looked like a racehorse. Many of the show horses I had known had been racehorses prior to their show days.

Before I could say anything to him, Nugget's golden face was nose-to-nose with me. His white blaze complimented a white forelock that was much shorter and better-groomed than Slippy's, and his mane lay evenly on the right side of his neck.

I was barely able to say hello to him before Noble Road pushed into my space. He was at least sixteen hands and had an angular look, usually seen in yearlings and two-year-olds, but he wasn't young. His coat was a dull brown and his black mane was so sparse that it stood on end, and he had no forelock at all.

I didn't get a chance to say a word before a delicate, dark face rubbed against my left jaw. "I'm Star Shadow."

She had a white star on her forehead, like mine, and she wasn't short, but she was slight and fit. Her dappled bay coat shone in the sunlight. She looked like a miniature racehorse.

Tom Jones' Roman nose needed no introduction, and he gave me a friendly nip on the neck before Kaiser pushed him out of the way.

I was surprised Kaiser hadn't shown up earlier, but I recognized his almost-black face right away. Kaiser let out a squeal, extended his right front leg straight out between us, and slammed his hoof to the ground—*thud*. I wasn't sure what that was supposed to mean.

Yellow Dog and Smokey stood off to the side as if waiting their turn. I didn't notice them until the constant talking eased off.

The horses had all been talking at once, and I couldn't understand much. The first one to walk away was Shorty, and within a few minutes the others wandered off to graze on the hay that lay loose in the field. Flakes of hay were spread far apart, and each horse picked out a spot to munch. Once they began to eat, my newness seemed to disappear.

I approached Smokey. He lifted his head. "Hello."

"Hi, I'm Big Guy. I'm new here."

"I heard." Smokey dropped his head and went back to his hay. "So you were a show horse?"

"Yes, I competed in hunter and hunt seat equitation

divisions."

"I used to do rodeo, speed-and-action." Smokey arched his neck with pride.

I had no idea what speed-and-action meant, but I had heard the rodeo was a cowboy horse show.

I then saw Paper Moon, who was grazing just beyond Smokey. When I walked over she lifted her head and stepped away.

"I just came over to say hello."

"Well, say it from there, please." She took another step back.

"I'm Big Guy, the new school horse."

"I'm Paper Moon, an old school horse."

Paper Moon was nearly white, with little dark flecks on her coat. I'd heard George call that color flea-bitten gray. She was lean, almost too lean, and there was a slight sway in her back. George used to sing a song about The Old Gray Mare, and I wondered if he had been singing about Paper Moon.

"I just wanted to introduce myself."

"And you did. Thank you, it was nice to meet you." Paper Moon took a few more steps away and began to graze.

I stood there wondering what I had done to offend her, but then I remembered Brownie. How could I have forgotten about Brownie? Where was Brownie?

I walked further into the field and saw, at the base of a gradual slope, a small stream. Brownie was near the water, grazing on the last green grass of the season. I nickered and trotted toward him. He lifted his head and took a square stance, all four legs spread. He was ready for anything. I knew from my youth that Brownie may be small and cute but he had a tornado swirling inside, and if I wanted to fight he would be ready.

"Remember me? I knew you when I was just a foal."

Brownie's stance didn't change.

"You're Brownie, Our-Dear-Precious-Little-Brownie—I grew up with you."

Brownie didn't move, and I slowed to a walk. "Come on, you remember me. You were turned out with a bunch of mares and foals. I was Copper Harbor's foal."

I thought I saw a glint of recognition, but his stance didn't change, so I stopped at a safe distance.

"When we were weaned you were our babysitter,"

"Do you have any idea how many foal crops I baby-sat in my years on that breeding farm?" Brownie didn't move.

I stood there, trying to think of something to remind Brownie of who I was. Of course he wouldn't remember me. There were ten foals in the field that year. I guess he saw foals year after year. Why did I think he would remember me?

I turned and walked back up the slope, found some hay that would allow me to see Brownie as I ate, and watched him grazing the green strip next to the water. Why was I so disappointed that he didn't remember me?

Chapter 9

LONG, BORING STORIES

"So, when you were horse-showing, did you travel much?" Yellow Dog was eating a flake of hay a few feet away.

I had never heard anyone call it horse-showing; we went to horse shows, we didn't go horse-showing. It sounded as strange as if he'd said he was hay-eating. I guess that's cowboy talk.

"I traveled the show circuit all but a couple months of the year. By the time I got to the National Finals at Madison Square Garden in November, I was tired of all that time in and out of horse trailers," I told him.

"Yeah, I didn't like being pushed in with all the other horses and standing for hours and hours. The only way to keep your balance was to lean on one another," he said.

"What are you talking about?" I had never heard of such a thing. "The only trailers and vans I ever saw had a separate stall for each horse; the stalls were so skinny we could barely back into them, but we could balance by leaning on the walls."

"You traveled in style." Yellow Dog laughed. "We were put in stock trailers loose, and everybody figured out where to stand and how to help each other out when the road was rough. Sometimes I got so hungry on the road," he added.

"We always had big nets full of hay hanging in front of us." I couldn't imagine traveling without snacks.

Yellow Dog yammered about a rodeo contest where he had to race across the arena and run through a little opening in a circle painted on the ground, spin around without stepping out of the circle, and race back. "The best time wins. I was pretty good at key-hole, but my specialty was barrel racing," he said proudly.

I had seen a lot of barrels in my life but couldn't imagine how a horse could race with one. I wondered if they laid the barrel on its side and rolled it down a hill. Was it judged on who got to the bottom first? I didn't care enough to ask, but Yellow Dog explained anyway.

"They set up three barrels in a triangle; one on the left, one on the right, and the third in the middle, further up the arena. I had to race out of the timer box, circle round the barrel on the left, then the right, then up the center to the last barrel, and race back. Best time wins, but you can't knock a barrel over. The shape you make when you run like that is a cloverleaf. That's why some people call it 'cloverleaf' instead of barrel racing."

I'm no longer listening, but Yellow Dog keeps talking. *I wished Brownie would talk to me.*

"The secret is to lean in around the barrel so you can keep up your speed, but you have to be far enough away so you don't bump the barrel with your shoulder. Sometimes I leaned so hard I almost fell down, but I was fast, brother, I was so fast," he continued.

Yellow Dog had no idea how little I cared about what he was saying, and I was surprised to find myself asking, "Did you win ribbons or trophies?"

"Sometimes it was ribbons or trophies, or belt buckles; the best was when we won money. Jeb, my person back then, loved it when we won money. I got apples and extra grain when money was the prize."

"I wonder what happened to old Jeb," he said.

"Why did you stop going to rodeo shows?" I wondered why I asked.

"They're not rodeo shows—they're rodeos." Yellow Dog dropped his head back to his hay. "I got old and didn't win as much."

Yellow Dog and I have more in common than I'd thought. I'm too old to win at the big shows and here I am, next to this horse who won't stop yammering, watching Brownie grazing by himself.

Yellow Dog kept talking. "I was sold to a little boy who did barrel racing at 4-H fairs and little local shows. He didn't let me go fast enough to win, most of the time. I could have won all those contests, but he never let me go all-out."

I let my ears droop to the side like wings, hoping Yellow Dog would notice that I wasn't paying attention, but he kept talking. "Justin wasn't the best rider, but he was good to me. He kept me groomed and well fed, and talked to me like I was a person. I heard about all his troubles, and sometimes about good things too." Yellow Dog hesitated. "He never said good-bye. A trailer showed up one day and brought me here, and I never saw him again."

Nancy had disappeared before I was moved to the school barn. She hadn't been there for weeks. I'd been sure something had happened to her, but now I wondered.

"Most of the school horses are here because they can't show or rodeo or whatever anymore," Yellow Dog added. "Some are here because their owners went away, or grew up, or just got tired of them. We're like a bunch of old leather halters whose brass buckles and rings are worn and dull—too good to throw away, but not good enough anymore," he said.

I was wearing a halter like the one Yellow Dog described. It had replaced my shiny show halter the morning I was moved to the school-horse barn. My ears drooped again, and it had nothing to do with Yellow Dog's chatter.

Chapter 10

The Life of a School Horse

"Are you all right?" I looked up. Yellow Dog was gone. Shorty asked again, "Are you all right?"

"Yeah, I guess so. I was thinking about what it's going to be like to be a school horse."

"Don't let Yellow Dog get you down. He's been here for over a year, and he's still mad at—what's his name, now?—Justin. I don't like to be mean but I think he needs to get over it."

Shorty's soft eyes reminded me of my mother again, and I asked, "How long have you been a school horse?"

"I've been here most of my life, and I'm twenty years old. We get good feed and clean stalls, and we don't work that hard. We get plenty of exercise, but we don't jump over big fences or get ridden more than a couple of hours a day. It's better than some stories I've heard," she said.

"Look at Paper Moon, over there." Shorty tipped her head toward Paper Moon and Smokey grazing side by side. "Jane bought her when another farm was going out of business. I heard Jane say she was afraid of what might happen to that paper-thin mare.

"That's how Paper Moon got her name. Jane said that all of the school horses at the sale were underweight, and some of them had saddle sores and old, untreated injuries." Shorty's eyes glowed. "I love to listen in on human conversations. They have no idea we can understand them. Don't you find that amusing?" she asked but didn't stop for my answer. "Jane said she needed a new school horse, and Paper Moon wasn't her first choice but she was worried a horse that skinny wouldn't attract a buyer and she'd end up at an auction. I guess auctions are not where any of us want to go,"

"Paper Moon does look pretty thin." I had wondered about that. "Everyone else looks well fed."

"Jane says she's white as paper and almost as thin."

Could that explain her rudeness this morning? Was Paper Moon afraid I might take her hay?

"She's gained weight in the last two months," Shorty said. "I could spare some weight, if she wanted it," she chuckled.

"I think you're the perfect weight." I let my nose touch her neck.

Shorty nibbled at the few bits of green November grass. "When Paper Moon arrived she had patches where her scabby skin oozed yellow liquid. Jane bathed her and treated it every day. It took a while for the fur to grow back, but you can hardly see where it was now.

"You see, Big Guy, the life of a school horse may not be glamorous, but we get good care here and I like my job,"

Shorty said. "Many of my riders bring me treats and tell me stories. They come and go, but some of them come back to see me long after they stop taking lessons. I've been here long enough for my students to bring their children for lessons, and they're surprised to see me still here."

"Wouldn't you rather be with one person or a family?" I asked.

Shorty lifted her head and looked me in the eye. "Would that be better than this? Children grow up and people move away, but I'm here when they decide to come back."

I looked at the horses around me. They weren't as shiny as the show horses, but they were groomed regularly. Their whiskers were long and I wondered what it was going to feel like to have the hair in my ears grow thick.

"Hey, Big Guy, are you in there?" Kaiser's face was right in front of me.

"You drifted off again." Shorty stood next to him.

"I was wondering why none of us have rear shoes on. I've been barefoot, but never half-way." I didn't want to tell them I was thinking about how shabby the school horses look, and I was curious about why none of the school horses wore rear shoes. I'd never heard of such a thing.

"That's so we don't hurt one another if we get in a scuffle out here. That happens once in a while," Kaiser said.

"Scuffles mostly caused by you." Shorty gave him a look.

"We need front shoes to work in the sand ring and go for cross-country rides," Kaiser said. "But we can do without rear shoes most of the time."

While he talked, I couldn't help looking at Kaiser's hairy ears. Shorty's were even furrier.

"What are you looking at?" Kaiser asked.

"I was wondering what it will be like to have hairy ears and long whiskers."

"That's the way it's supposed to be." Kaiser flicked his ears toward me. "These hairy guys keep the flies and mosquitoes out in the summer, and keep me warmer in the winter. You better hope your ears grow in thick before the cold weather hits. We spend a lot more time outside than you show horses. That much time indoors would drive me nuts."

I looked toward the show barn and saw Taylor Maid being led back inside. I used to like talking to her. I missed her and Ding and Painted Doll. I missed Ding the most.

"Earth to Big Guy." Kaiser was shaking his head in front of me. "What are you thinking about now?"

"I was thinking about my friend Ding."

"That doesn't sound like a show name."

Kaiser's interest in names made me laugh.

"His show name is Battle's Image; his nickname is Ding."

"How'd he get that name?"

I didn't understand why Kaiser made such a big deal out of names. "I don't know, it's just what his person, Debbie, calls him," I said.

Brownie was nibbling nearby. His coat was thick, and tufts of hair stuck out of his ears. I wanted to talk to him. *He's right there and I could just say, "Hi, I'm sorry I bothered you this morning. I thought you would remember me."*

A whistle pierced the air and everyone lifted their heads and walked, trotted, then cantered toward the gate. I followed Brownie.

Each horse went back to its own stall without being led. Jane walked next to me. "Being the last one in makes it easier for me to teach you how to do this. You simply walk back to your stall every night." She rested her hand on my neck but didn't attach the lead rope in her hand. "You'll have this routine down in no time."

While everyone ate their afternoon grain, I had time to think about how strange the day had been. My stablemates weren't exactly messy or dirty, but they were not nearly as well-groomed as the show horses. Why doesn't someone pull their manes and clean them up?

I would never look like a real show horse again.

Lady Bug walked into my stall and jumped up on my feed rack. I was glad to see her again. The school and show barns are near one another but I didn't know if she ever came up to the school horse barn.

"I was wondering where you were," she said

Do all cats sound like they know more than anyone on Earth about absolutely everything?

"I couldn't exactly ask them if I could bring my pet cat with me, could I?"

I lowered my nose and she brushed her body against my face.

"What are you doing up here, anyway?" She was pressing her forehead against mine.

"I'm not a show horse anymore. I couldn't cut it. I'm just an old school horse now," I said.

"Why so glum, chum? This barn looks good to me. I think there may be more mice to catch in here. The grain room is here; that should attract some prime hunting prospects," said Lady Bug looking around my stall.

"This wooden platform you eat off isn't as nice as your feed tub, but this could work for me." Lady Bug scratched at the wooden surface. "The stall's clean and the bedding's deep. I could snuggle down there next to you at night."

"Who's your friend?" Shorty asked.

"This is Lady Bug, she's a mouser from the show barn."

"I didn't think they allowed mice in the hoity-toity show barn." Kaiser put his nose in the air.

"You might be surprised," Lady Bug said. "If you know how to hunt, there's always prey available."

"I'm glad I don't eat meat," I said. "I don't think I'd like to kill my food."

"It would be against your nature," Lady Bug said. "I can eat cat food if I want to, but I could hunt for my food and take care of myself in the wild. I think you'd starve on your own, Big Guy."

There it is again—cat arrogance. As much as I like Lady Bug, she can be annoying.

I slept comfortably that night, resting my nose in the soft bedding next to Lady Bug.

Chapter 11

The Feed Room

"Do you want to know what's behind the door opposite the tack room?" Slippy's big bay head seemed to appear from nowhere. The rest of the horses were grazing around us.

"I hadn't thought about it." I was out in the pasture almost every day now; getting to know my stablemates was easier than it had been in the show barn, where we could only talk from stall to stall.

"I heard Shorty tell you about the tack room the other night," Slippy said. "So I thought you'd like to know what's behind the door on the other side of the aisle."

"You know what's in there?" I was intrigued.

"It's the feed room. There are bags full of sweet feed in there, stacked higher than my withers."

"I thought I could smell the molasses, corn, and oats when the door was left open," Slippy said. "One day, when a little boy was walking me back to the barn after a lesson,

I dragged the little kid through the door. The wheelbarrow full of grain was next to the stacked-up bags, and I got to eat grain until Jane found us. She doesn't leave that door open anymore."

Slippy told me stories about working with a circus and pulling a chuck wagon in a race at a rodeo. His stories were more interesting than Yellow Dog's. Maybe he was a better storyteller. I didn't know what a homemade beer wagon was, but it sounded like he had fun pulling it in parades.

"Isn't being a school horse a letdown after doing all that interesting stuff?"

"Are you kidding?" he replied. "This is easy work, with good feed and clean stalls. I had to travel a lot with the circus and rodeo; sometimes the places we stayed were nice, sometimes they were awful. Being a school horse isn't as boring as I'd thought it would be, and if I get bored, I have ways of changing things up."

"What do you mean?"

"You'll see." Slippy laughed and walked away.

Chapter 12

Test Ride as a School Horse

"Hey, Big Guy, how would you like to go for a little spin?" Jane unhooked the chain behind my stall and moved up to my head on my left side, letting one hand slide along my body as she went. With the brush in her right hand, curry in her left, Jane talked and groomed with the same efficiency George had used.

"You're the tallest school horse I've ever had. Many of my students will only be able to reach up to here. She set the brush halfway up my shoulder. "Your legs and stomach will be well groomed."

After she'd gone over my body and combed through my mane and tail, Jane set the saddle in place, brought the girth up to a slight snug, and slid a bridle over my head. "Nancy told me that this snaffle bit will work just fine for you. I like to use the mildest bit I can on school horses. Some of your riders aren't going to be as light with their hands as you're used to. The students I put on you won't be beginners, but they won't have the years of experience Nancy had. Not every horse can make it as a school horse."

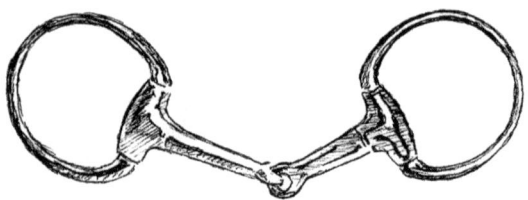

As a schoolie, I'm going to have to put up with riders tugging at my mouth day after day? I knew being a school horse would be a step down from being a show horse, but I hadn't thought about the prospect of clumsy hands on my reins.

Jane led me into the arena, stopping to tighten the girth before walking me up to the mounting block, a little wooden box on the ground so that kids can step up to reach the stirrup.

Jane stood on the wooden box beside me, but instead of taking up the reins and stepping into the left stirrup, she turned around, touched her toes, turned toward me again, unzipped her jacket, took it off, put it back on, and zipped it up again. Very confusing, but I figured she had her reasons.

"Nancy said you were a gentleman at the mounting block, but this is amazing," she said as she took up the reins and settled lightly onto my back. Then she stepped off again.

"Sorry for the test Big Guy but some of your riders might do things that experienced riders never do, like shaking a jacket around or dragging their toe over your back, instead of swinging their leg over cleanly. I know this is unfair, Big Guy, but there are some things I need to know."

She stepped back into the left stirrup, and as she swung her right leg over my back, she let her toe drag across my rump. That felt weird, but not enough to make me do more than hump my back.

Settled into the saddle, Jane asked me to step away from the mounting block. We walked around the little arena on a long rein. I could let my head and neck relax as we warmed up slowly.

There were two indoor riding arenas attached like an L. The big arena was usually full of jumps. The little arena often had no jumps at all, but today it held five small fences.

We walked, trotted, and cantered with Jane commenting often. "What a lovely long trot you have. This might bounce a beginner off, but more advanced riders are going to love it."

We cantered across the arena, and Jane signaled a lead change as I approached the center of the ring. Sometimes the timing for the lead change makes no sense to me, but I change on signal whether it makes sense or not. Jane patted my neck again. "I have some students who are going to love you, Big Guy."

We walked up to a fence that had two vertical rails. Jane jumped down and took the left end of the top rail and set it on the ground. She lifted the other rail to the upper cup and set the right side on the ground. She'd created a cross pole, which had been my standard warm-up fence since I began jumping. Jane mounted from the ground. I wondered why she didn't go to the mounting block; it wasn't far away. She made some funny noises but managed to get her left foot into the stirrup. "Who am I trying to impress? Next time, to the mounting block."

We trotted to the cross pole and I hopped over the little X and cantered away. I had done this so many times, I could do it in my sleep. The courses in the show ring required jumping eight or ten fences in a specific order, but the warm-ups always started with going back and forth over a cross pole. At the bigger shows, the courses could be longer and more complicated, and the height of the fences may be challenging.

After a few cross pole warm-ups, we trotted the X, and then cantered to a tiny vertical. It was a simple two rails, less than three feet high. I had jumped fences like this when I was just learning to jump. We trotted the X to the vertical again, then around the corner to another small vertical, and took five easy strides to a three-foot oxer. This fence had another rail in the back, a little higher than the front, making the jump wider.

"You are a joy." We walked into the big arena, where I usually worked, Jane patting my neck. "I wasn't going to do this, but I can't resist."

We trotted into a gymnastic line that began with a series of three cross poles with no stride in between: jump, land, jump, land, jump. I took a single stride to a three-foot vertical, then two strides to a three-foot-six oxer that was about three feet wide. I was anticipating a much longer workout, but Jane brought me to a walk and said, "I could do this all day, but I don't think you need training and I want to use you for a lesson this afternoon. My students are going to love the new school horse."

That's it? That's my whole workout? The fences were small; it had taken little effort, and we were finished before I thought we'd begun. I could get used to this.

We cooled off by walking down the road. "You are a joy to ride, Big Guy. I was worried that you might be too much horse for some of my students, and too tall for many of them, but I think you're going to be quite useful in the school horse string."

A car drove toward us, and I sidled to the edge of the road. Jane patted my neck. "I guess you haven't been on the road much. That car won't hurt you."

A truck rattled past and I found myself on top of a bank next to the road. Jane laughed. "I guess we have this to work on. Trucks can be scary, can't they?" She patted my neck again. "I'm sure we'll get past this. I think you're going to have a fan club."

Chapter 13

LITTLE LISA

A little girl appeared behind me. "Hi! You're the new horse. Do you mind if I come in and visit?"

Does she think I have a choice?

She barely had to duck to get under the rump chain behind me, and her blonde head passed just above my knee. *Do they let babies take lessons around here?* She patted the top of my front leg, then scrambled up onto the wooden deck where I eat my hay and grain. When she stood on the deck, her freckles and braids were at eye level.

"I'm Lisa, and I'm five years old. I'm too little to take lessons yet, but when I'm seven I can start. My sister Angie is eight, and she's taking her lesson right now."

Kaiser banged his rump against the wall. I thought he might give it a kick, but he didn't.

"That's Kaiser. Angie likes to ride him, but today she's riding Golden Boy. Jane lets them pick the horse they want, but she doesn't let them ride one horse all the time. I don't know why. I would pick you."

She was patting my neck, my muzzle, smoothing my forelock. I don't usually like strangers rubbing my ears, but she moved so gently that it felt good to have her stroke my ears, with her thumb inside and fingers outside. She started at the base of my ear, then moved up to the tip, and started over again.

"Some horses don't like this but I think it would feel good. Don't you? I do this for my dog Max, and he loves it. Sometimes he drools. Do horses ever drool?"

Kaiser bumped the wall again and Shorty stomped one hoof the way my mother used to when I didn't behave. I thought she was telling Kaiser to mind his manners.

"That's Shorty. When I start lessons, Angie says I'll ride her first because she's little and easy. She has pretty eyes too. I brushed her last week."

Little Lisa looked me straight in the eye. "You're the biggest horse I've ever seen. Your eyes are pretty and your eyelashes are long, but you don't have any long pokey hairs around your eyes like the other horses. It makes your eyes look prettier. You don't have any whiskers around your mouth either, and your nose is soft."

Even a child can see the importance of good grooming.

"When I grow up, I'm going to have a horse like you," Lisa said. "He's going to be big and pretty and I'm going to take care of him every day."

Little Lisa pulled a body brush out of her jacket pocket; it was smaller than any brush I'd ever seen. "My mom got this for me because my hands are small."

She swept the tiny brush along the fur on my face, jaw,

and neck. "I like grooming horses. Angie says that horses like being groomed. Do you like this?"

She moved the brush under my jaw and brushed toward my chin. I must say that having the underside of my jaw groomed is one of my favorite spots. The student who groomed me earlier today had ignored that spot completely. That student had worked like she was in a hurry, but Little Lisa took her time and her tiny brush fit perfectly into the groove between my cheekbones. Her grooming style was soft and kind. Horse show grooms move efficiently and never miss a spot. They use quick little sweeps along my jawline and it feels good, but not as good as this tiny girl with the miniature brush.

Little Lisa talked as she played with my mane and forelock. "My dad said he would get me a horse if I learn how to ride and get good grades and behave myself. Angie said she doesn't think he'll ever do it, but I know she's wrong."

She started to rub my ears again and I

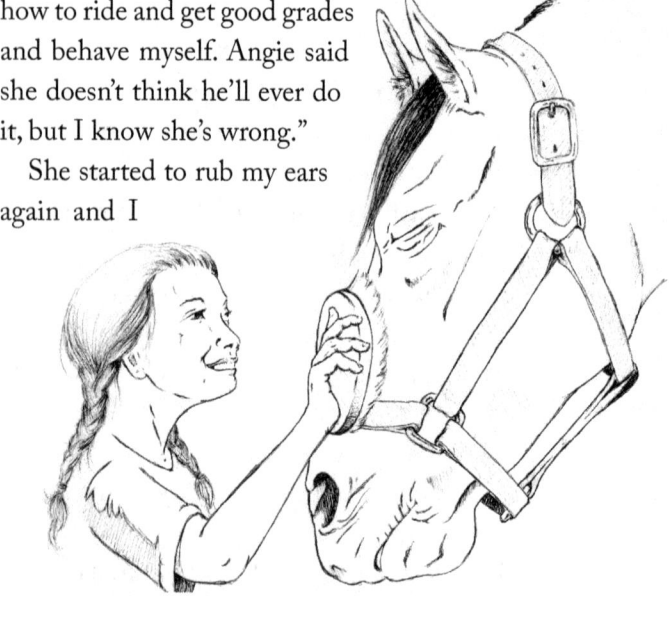

dropped my head so she could reach them easier. My nose rested on her feet.

"Angie started taking lessons when her friend Kim did. Angie likes to ride all right, but she doesn't like horses the way I do. She just wants to do stuff with her mean friend. Kim isn't mean most of the time, but sometimes she makes me cry. She calls me Tag Along and Rug Rat and stuff like that, just because I'm little. Someday I'll be big and I'll show her."

Lesson horses clip-thump-clop-thumped into the barn. "Well, I've got to go. Angie's lesson is over. I'll come back and see you next week."

She sat on the edge of the wooden deck, dropped to the floor, and began to brush my legs and stomach. "Does this feel good? Max loves it when I rub his tummy."

"Lisa, it's time to go."

"That's Angie, she's my sister, but I already told you that."

"Come on, Rug Rat, we're going to get ice cream."

"That's Kim. She's feeling mean today, but ice cream usually makes her nicer." Lisa patted the top of my front leg and gave it a kiss. "I love you, Big Guy."

"Aw, ain't that cute?" Kaiser said after they left.

"It is cute." Shorty sounded like she was about to cry. "That's one of the nice things about being a school horse, Big Guy. There are so many children who love us and bring us treats and tell us stories."

"Don't get all drippy-eyed, Shorty. She'll be in love with another horse in a few minutes."

"Kaiser, you have children who always want to ride you because you're their favorite. They bring you treats and tell you stories too," Shorty said.

"Then they go off to college or get married and I never see them again. Don't fall for it, Big Guy, they don't really mean it."

I thought about Nancy and how many times she had groomed and talked to me. And now she's gone and I'm in a slip stall wondering what it would be like if Little Lisa were my person.

Chapter 14

MY HERD

After weeks in the field, I'd discovered how much I enjoyed being outside with my herd. Shorty and Kaiser are often nearby, Yellow Dog drops by to chat, and Brownie makes a point of ignoring me. On this late fall day, we had eaten all the hay in the first hour or two, then spread out to nibble at spent strands of brown grass. There's not much worth eating this late in November, but the act of grazing is soothing.

Why is everyone moving? We eat and amble often, but now we're all moving toward the far fence.

"Is he going to do it again?" Kaiser asked.

"That's what it looks like." *Was Shorty laughing?*

"What's he doing, and who are you talking about?" I asked.

"Slippy's an escape artist." Shorty was definitely laughing.

"And when he breaks out, we all break out," Kaiser said as we came to a standstill.

"Watch and learn, boy." Kaiser's ears pricked forward. "Slippy looks for weak areas in the fencing, then uses that massive chest of his to strain that weakness to the breaking point."

Slippy leaned on the woven-wire fence, and I heard the sound of wire snapping. The rectangles of wire in front of Slippy were bending.

"Can he just walk through a fence like that?" I'd never thought about breaking through a fence.

"No, he found a spot where two pieces of fence were repaired with weak twists of wire. Slippy can spot a sloppy patch-job, and we all get to take advantage of his skill." Kaiser seemed envious of the talent.

Snap. Snap.

Slippy lifted his right front hoof and pressed what remained of the fence to the ground, and another snap followed. When his left hoof stepped onto the fence, two more wires snapped and what was left of the fence was crushed to the weedy ground. Everyone filed through after him.

I held back, not sure what to think. I had never been outside of a fenced enclosure, but they were going to walk away. I stepped through the gap and felt the wires moving under my feet. It felt strange and I backed up. *Maybe I don't want to go with them.*

My right front hoof was caught in the fence. I took two steps back and the remains of the fence pulled itself up out of the matted grass. I was trapped. I pulled harder and the fence followed me—it was after me! I backed up until the fence that was still attached to a post stopped me. My hoof was in the air, my leg stretched in front of me, and I couldn't get away.

"I'm stuck! The fence got me!"

Kaiser stood a few feet away. "Settle down, Big Guy, you're making it worse. Don't back up, walk forward. The fence is caught between your hoof and your front shoe." Kaiser's calm voice helped, but not much. I stepped forward and the fence settled back to the ground.

"You've always had fancy wooden fences, haven't you?" Kaiser didn't seem to understand that I was trapped. I stepped back again and the fence came with me.

"Stop that." Kaiser looked over his shoulder at the horses walking away.

"Walk forward until you're on top of the wire, then lift the hoof that's stuck and shake it back and forth."

I moved forward and shook my hoof, like he said. The fence shook but it didn't let go of me. I shook harder and stepped back.

"Don't back up," Kaiser shouted. "Step forward and shake that hoof. Be patient; the wire will slide out, the same way it slid in. Just keep calm and follow my directions."

"How do you know this will work?" I shook my hoof harder.

"I grew up in Montana, where every fence is wire: woven wire, barbed wire, electric wire, every wire combination you can imagine. I've seen and done this before. Just relax and—"

My hoof came loose and the wire dropped to the ground, but I was afraid to move.

"Step high over that downed wire," Kaiser said.

I picked my feet up as high as I could.

"There you go, Big Guy, now let's catch up." Kaiser was trotting away, and I followed.

We caught up and settled into a trot. I was part of a herd. I hadn't felt like this since I was a foal. When Slippy got to a dirt road, he turned right and we moved from a trot to a canter. Within a few strides we were galloping. Ten horses and a pony—*how could Brownie keep up?*
He was right there, ears flat back, hooves pounding the packed gravel road. I felt like a wild animal.

A truck rounded the corner in front of us, bigger than any truck I had ever seen. It stopped; we didn't. I wasn't sure what the truck might do, but I didn't have time to think about it. The driver's eyes were wide, his mouth open. My herd parted without hesitation, barely missing the truck's mirrors, and zipped down the road. I had never run this fast and hard. I felt like I could run forever.

Slippy turned sharply in front of us and we slowed and trotted onto a flat green pasture. How could the grass be this green so late in the year? We milled about for a few minutes, then began to graze. The grass was as sweet as June, and we were grazing like we had never eaten before.

"Don't drink that stuff," Shorty said. I was walking toward a pond.

"I'm thirsty."

"Let him try it. He won't do it twice." Kaiser nudged me toward the water.

I wasn't sure if I was thirsty anymore, but I wanted to taste the water. It looked clear and cold, and I sucked in a mouthful. "*Phft*—what is that stuff?"

"It's a swimming pool." Kaiser laughed.

"In the summer, during day camp, we'll be ridden to the big house where the campers swim and eat their lunch. They turn us out in the field next to the pool and we can watch them." It sounded like Shorty enjoyed going to the pool.

"Is this the big house?" I looked toward the house near the pond.

"No, the big house is further away." Shorty looked over her shoulder. "We go through the woods to get there."

My herd was spread over the beautiful green pasture when Jane walked up carrying a lead rope. "All right, you guys, the party's over."

She grabbed Shorty's halter and tied the rope to the rings on each side, creating a makeshift bridle. She hopped on Shorty's back and began to walk away, looking over her shoulder like she expected us to follow. "Playing hard to get, are we?"

Jane turned around, walked back to Slippy, and grabbed his halter with her left hand. "Why do I think this was your idea?"

She walked around us and began to trot away. That got our attention; we were behind her, trotting toward the road. Jane looked over her shoulder, let go of Slippy, and urged Shorty into a canter. When we got to the road, the canter turned into a gallop. The trip back to the barn was almost as exciting as the escape had been.

"I hope we slow down before we get to the hole in the fence," I said.

"We won't be going back through the fence. We'll come in the front gate," Kaiser said.

He was right. We slowed to a canter before we turned

into the drive, passed the gates, and dropped back to a trot. Jane ducked down to Shorty's neck as she trotted into the barn, and took a few walking strides before she rode right into Shorty's stall.

We all slipped into our stalls as if we were coming in from a quiet afternoon in the pasture, but we were breathing heavily, thrilled with our adventure.

Chapter 15

Nancy Comes Back

Her pace slowed as she neared my stall and ducked under the chain behind me. "Hey, Big Guy, how are you doing?"

Nancy's back! Where has she been? Did she know what happened to me? She will straighten this out. I'm not supposed to be here—she'll fix it.

She stood next to me, patting my neck. *I knew she would come back for me.* "How's life as a school horse working out for you?"

*What do you mean 'life as a school horse'? I'm not a school horse, I'm **your** horse. I've been your horse for years and you need to fix this. Take me back to my box stall.* I wished she could hear what I was saying.

"I'm sorry, but I think this is the best thing for you, Big Guy. I know how hard you were trying, and you just couldn't compete at the big shows anymore. Your arthritis is getting worse." She hugged my neck. "I didn't want to sell you, but

Dad said we couldn't board two horses and this seemed like the best thing to do." Her tears left a wet spot on my neck. She knew what had happened; she had decided to do this to me. *How could she throw me away like this?*

"I didn't give you away. You still belong to me, but I thought life as a school horse would be good for you. You'll get regular exercise but you won't have to work so hard. You won't jump big fences or be in trailers for hours and hours between shows. You can go outside and be with other horses. The vet said this would be better for your arthritis. You can live like a real horse instead of a show horse."

What do you mean by 'real horse'? Show horses are real horses. School horses are has-beens. Some of these guys never were anything but school horses—they're not even has-beens, they're never-weres. If Nancy could only hear me, she would understand.

I lifted the peppermint candy from her hand. How many times had she walked back to the barn next to me while I ate this treat, and she always said the same thing, "Now your breath is minty-fresh."

She kicked the bedding at my feet. "Your stall will be nice and clean. I know Jane will take good care of you, and I'll be around if anything goes wrong. You're still my Big Guy, and you always wi—"

"Nancy, the van from Canada is here," her father called from outside.

"Sorry, Big Guy, gotta go." Her boot heels clicked as she ran out of the barn.

I waited for Kaiser to say something. He had an opinion, I was certain of that, but he didn't speak. Shorty, sweet

Shorty, she would have words of consolation, but she quietly munched on her hay. I tipped my head so I could see Kaiser's eye, but he turned away without a word. Shorty was my best bet for sympathy, but when I caught her eye she kept eating in silence, like she didn't see me.

"So what do you guys think? I know you heard what Nancy said. Come on, Kaiser, spit it out."

"Yes, I heard Nancy." Kaiser showed his left eye through the gap in the boards. "And I heard what she didn't hear. Why would you want my opinion? I'm a has-been."

I didn't look at Shorty, but she spoke up. "You're wise not to look my way. I'm one of those never-weres."

Chapter 16

Brownie

Trotting out of the barn and cantering to our pasture, I was with my herd again. Through the gate and spread out to browse on the hay strewn around—I felt like I'd been doing this all my life. But no one spoke to me. They grazed with their rumps toward me. Even Yellow Dog avoided me.

I ate my hay in silence. Brownie was eating hay with us, the green grass near the stream had gone brown. When the hay was gone we continued to hunt for every sprig. I looked at Shorty, hoping she would say something. She glanced my way, then dropped her head, more interested in half-dead grass.

I could hear them talking among themselves. The group walked down past the stream to graze the sunny slope beyond. Usually there's conversation before such a move, but I wasn't included. I followed at a distance, and found Brownie walking next to me. "You blew it, Big Guy."

"I know, I shouldn't have said it." Brownie hadn't spoken to me since my first day with the herd.

"They know what you think of them."

"But I like them. I like being in this herd," I said.

"That's not what they heard you say yesterday."

"I was upset. I didn't understand how Nancy could give me up like that. I was trying to think of ways to change her mind and now . . . they hate me." I was trying to convince Nancy to take me back, and I ruined the herd I had just begun to fit in with.

"They think you think you're better than them," Brownie said.

"But you don't think that."

Brownie gave his head a shake, his thick mane flopping from side to side. "I've been around longer than any horse here. Ponies live forever—at least it seems that way. I've been stabled with racehorses, show horses, school horses, circus horses . . ."

"Circus horses?" I wondered if he had circus stories, like Slippy.

"That one always gets attention. Circus horses are just like the rest of us. There are stars, and the ones who pull the wagons and they're all just horses. We're all just horses."

"But you're a tough guy."

"I'm no tougher than Kaiser, and he's a wimp. It's a show. I'm short, so I act big. Kaiser's weak, so he acts strong." Brownie dropped his head to graze. "Let's stop here for a while.

"They were starting to respect you," he said. "You're big, that's an advantage, and you're quiet. Real strength usually is."

I didn't feel strong.

"They're disappointed; they were starting to trust you. Now, they're not so sure."

"How can I fix this?" There must be something I could say or do; something that would change their minds.

"You can't take back your words. You have to wait until they have time to see who you are again. You'll prove yourself."

"Until then I'm going to be pretty lonely. Why are you talking to me now, when you wouldn't before?"

"I've been where you are. When I first got here and saw that I was the only pony, I acted tough and kicked a few horses pretty hard. I'd thought I was defending myself but I was making enemies.

We all make mistakes, say and do stupid things. They know that too. That's why this will go away, eventually," he said, munching next to me.

"Until then, we can be buddies."

I looked up the hill at the herd that didn't want me. The two of us grazed. Brownie didn't talk much, but I had to ask him, "Do you remember my mother?"

"Copper Harbor wasn't big like you, but she had a big heart and she was calm. You got your easy-going manner from her."

"So you do remember me." I couldn't believe it.

"No, you were one of the foals—they came and went. But, the mares I got to know over the years, and Copper Harbor was one of the best."

I lifted my head to a spot where the sun shone through tree branches, warming my face. "She was beautiful too," I said.

"Let's get up on this slope and into the sun. Follow me." Brownie moved up the hill. "We'll walk right into the middle of the herd and take our place. They'll move away, but we'll keep doing that until they get over what you said. Besides, I want to lay down up there and soak up some rays."

I felt odd following Brownie, a tiny butterscotch-colored pony followed by a huge shadow. The other horses moved away as Brownie pushed his way into the herd and began to graze among them. Kaiser walked away. Shorty glanced my way but chose not to speak. Yellow Dog lifted his head as if to say something, but changed his mind. I tried to ignore them but knew I was the one being ignored. When Brownie lay down to soak up the sun, I did the same. It was unusually warm for December.

Closing my eyes was a relief. I couldn't see them, and I could pretend to be sleeping and look calm and relaxed, though that wasn't how I felt. How was I ever going to fit in again? I woke up when Brownie scrambled to his feet. I must have been out for quite a while; the rest of the herd had moved to the far side of the field. Brownie and I grazed for a few minutes, then he moved off toward the herd, with me, his oversized shadow following.

Brownie usually grazed along the edge of the group, but today, every time they moved to a new site, he pushed himself into the center. Horses often move as they graze, but I felt like they were trying to leave me behind on purpose.

"Are they trying to get away from me?" I said quietly to Brownie.

"They always move like this. I think you're being paranoid." Brownie didn't care if the rest of the herd heard him.

By the end of the day they didn't pull away as much, except for Kaiser. He stepped away if I got anywhere near him. When Jane whistled at the gate, Shorty was grazing next to me. "Afternoon grain and then—lesson time, here we come."

Was she talking to me? I think Shorty was talking me. She usually said something like that almost every day, but now I was pleased to think she was saying it to me.

"Back to the grind," I said.

Shorty didn't respond. Maybe she wasn't talking to me. *You should have kept your mouth shut, Big Guy.* But she was walking next to me the way she usually does back to the barn. *Say something, Big Guy—something funny, or cute, or anything. What if she wasn't talking to me? What if I say something stupid?*

Back inside, the sound of ten horses eating grain filled the barn.

Chapter 17

Switcheroo

"What's going on?" I was in Kaiser's stall and he was in mine.

"I don't know, she put me in here on purpose." Kaiser must have forgotten that he wasn't talking to me.

Jane ducked under the chain behind my stall and poured grain on the plank platform in front of me. When she did the same for Kaiser, she said, "Kaiser I'm tired of picking up saddles every morning. I don't know why you knock them down every night, but you won't be able to do it from here."

As she ducked into Shorty's stall, she said, "Why didn't I think of this before?"

"It looks like this is permanent, Kaiser." I could hardly hear Shorty, one stall farther away.

The herd was talking to me again, though cautiously. Kaiser was the only one who hadn't said a word to me for weeks. Yellow Dog was sharing his long, boring stories again. How could I have missed them? Brownie and I still grazed together often. Today I have a wall on my right and Kaiser, who may as well be a wall, on my left. I'll miss having Shorty so close.

"I don't like this stall." Kaiser was eating his grain and complaining. "My water bucket has a nice dent in it where I can set my jaw as I drink. A kid forgot to tie me in one day, and I turned around in my stall. When I got tired of looking at the aisle, I gave that bucket a good blast just to see what it would sound like."

"Jane heard that and came in here before you destroyed your own water bucket." *Why did Shorty sound so far away?*

"I like my customized bucket. Big Guy, yours has no character at all; just smooth and round."

"I'd gladly trade back." *He was talking to me!* But he went silent again. Maybe he remembered that he was mad at me.

Thump. "I was wondering when that would start." Shorty laughed when Kaiser started his evening wall-kicking. "What are you going to do when you don't hear the saddles fall?"

"This is going be far less satisfying. I may have to kick until I'm tired of it." *Thump.*

"Oh dear, I hate to think how long that might take." Shorty wasn't laughing now.

I offered to kick my wall until the saddles fell, and Shorty said, "Big Guy, you don't want to start a habit like that."

"I don't know if you have what it takes to hit the wall just right," Kaiser said. "I like to hear them fall one at a time. As big as you are, you might have them falling in one big thud. There are some things a guy just has to do for himself." *Thump.* He was definitely talking to me again.

Kaiser was accustomed to kicking with his right hind leg to smack against the tack room's wall. He occasionally switched to his left, but not very often. That night, when he switched legs, the *Thump* became a *Thunk*.

"I like the sound of that," Kaiser said. "I'm not hitting against a board, I'm smacking into a support beam." *Thunk*. "Yeah, that's a difference I could learn to like."

"Oh, dear me," Shorty said.

"Don't worry, Shorty, this won't take long. It won't be as satisfying as saddles falling, but I like the sound enough, I won't have to do it for too long."

"Thank goodness."

We grew accustomed to Kaiser's nightly *Thump* and *Thunk*, but something changed one night. The *Thunk* had a different tenor. "I think I loosened that board." *Thunkkk*. "Yeah, it's loose all right." *Thkkk*.

Kaiser wasn't kicking, he was thrashing. "My leg's stuck! My leg's stuck! My hoof is between the board and the beam, I think I'm caught on a nail."

"Oh dear, you're bleeding." Shorty could see more than I could.

Kaiser struggled and then stopped. "I got it out but it hurts—it hurts a lot."

"You're bleeding. Try not to move around too much," Shorty said.

"Is there anything I can do?" I couldn't see much.

"There's nothing to do but wait for the bleeding to stop." Kaiser sounded worried.

I thought that a human could help, but had no way to let them know what happened. Jane was in her apartment over the tack room, and wouldn't be back in the barn until the morning. I threw myself against one wall, then slammed my body against the other wall. I reared to my hind legs and struck at the front of my stall. Then did it all again.

Over the noise, I heard Shorty ask, "Big Guy, what are you doing?"

"If we make enough noise, Jane will hear us!"

Shorty started slamming around in her stall and the others did likewise. Slippy was making more noise than the rest of us.

"What is going on down here?" Jane stood behind me wearing her pajamas, a jacket, and tall black rubber boots. "You woke me out of a sound sleep. It sounds like you're all being stung by bees or—Oh my! Oh whoa—Kaiser, what have you done to yourself?"

When Dr. Loewith arrived near midnight, all the lights in the barn were on. Kaiser's leg was wrapped and waiting for the verdict on how badly injured he was.

Jane had talked to Kaiser as she'd tended to his wound.

"Kaiser, you old fool, it looks like you've almost taken

your hoof off. I stopped the bleeding, but can't do much more until the vet gets here." She'd wrapped a wet towel around his leg, then applied a polo wrap. "I'm sorry, buddy. I'll put you back in your old stall when this is over and *never* complain about picking up saddles again. This wouldn't have happened in your old stall. This is all my fault."

She stood up. "That looks better for now."

The vet left Kaiser in the stall while he worked, so I could hear everything and see some of what was going on.

"There's not much I can suture here. I'll sew the spot on the bulb of his heel, then wrap it up and hope for the best. You're right, Jane, he's cut just above the hoof almost all the way around. I don't hold much hope for how this will heal. We may end up calling the zoo on this one."

I had never heard of the zoo. *What's the zoo?*

"What do you mean, call the zoo?" Jane asked.

She doesn't know what a zoo is either.

"I can't close it up and it may not heal the way it should. If we do get it healed, it's likely to leave him very lame. If we ship him to the zoo on the hoof, they'll put him down for the big cats."

"Are you talking about feeding Kaiser to the cats?" Jane sounded shocked.

"Well, the cats and other large carnivores. They have to eat, you know, and this would be a lot of healthy protein to let go to waste."

I flashed on the image of our barn cat, Lady Bug, hunting mice and chipmunks. She waits and waits, then pounces and catches a mouse so fast. I didn't want to think about a big cat doing to Kaiser what Lady Bug does to those little mice. How big are the cats at the zoo?

"I understand the circle of life," Jane said. "I know how that works, but I'll do everything I can to avoid that phone call."

"You'll have some work ahead of you. I agree, it's too early to give up on him, but I want you to be aware that this may just fall apart. Even with the antibiotic this wound could get infected. Without infection, if everything goes just right, he may be too lame to be useful as a school horse or even to hobble around a pasture. I want you to be ready in case your efforts don't work."

"I understand. Can I walk him down to the lower barn to

keep him close to the wash rack? It will be easier to hose off his leg every day."

"Yes, hydrotherapy is going to be your best bet. Let cold water run over this wound for about fifteen minutes three or four times a day. Keep doing that until the wounds have closed. I'll stop and give it a look when I'm in the area, and you can call me with any questions." He patted Kaiser before he walked away. "Let's hope this works, fella."

Chapter 18

What's a Lion?

The next morning, Jane led me down to the show barn and put me in the stall next to Kaiser. I like the way she talks to me as if she knows I understand.

"Kaiser has to stay inside until he begins to heal. During the day, when the other horses are outside, I think he'll be happier if one of his stablemates is down here with him. Shorty can do this tomorrow, and you two will trade back and forth, so you can go outside every other day. Kaiser will be less bored with a buddy next door."

I'm Kaiser's buddy. He hated me for a while, now I'm his buddy.

After the school horses were turned out, Jane came down to the barn, unwrapped Kaiser's leg, and stood him in the wash rack for hydrotherapy.

I always liked going in the wash rack; I used to get baths there. After a hard workout, Nancy would lead me in, turn me around on the cement floor, and put me in the crossties.

Ropes hung from both sides of the wash rack, and with them clipped to either side of my halter, Nancy had both hands free to let cold water run over my legs while she patted my neck. That felt so good.

Jane talked to Kaiser as she let the water soothe his wound. "Kaiser, I don't like the amount of blood still oozing from that cut. I'll follow the vet's direction, but I think there's too much red in the water."

The water ran for a long time and Jane talked to Kaiser the whole time.

"Now you listen to me, mister—if you start kicking at the walls before this gets a chance to heal, I may have to call the zoo. I'm going to do my part, but you have to let this leg rest. Do you hear me? I wish you could understand what I'm saying."

She applied salve to his wounds and wrapped him up again. Back in the stall she leaned her head close to his. "Every time you want to kick at the wall, I want you to stop and think: *Lion Food*."

"What's a lion?" Kaiser asked.

I was hoping Kaiser had forgotten about his question from the day before yesterday, but he jumped on it as soon as I was in the stall next to him.

I didn't want to tell him. I wasn't certain I believed it. I shuffled my feet, trying to think of something to say that had nothing to do with lions. "Slippy was with a circus for a while, he pulled the wagons for the shows and parades."

"I know all that. What's a lion?"

"He exaggerates a lot and . . . um. So, how's your leg feeling?"

Kaiser stomped one front hoof. "Just tell me what he said."

"It may not be true . . ."

"Tell me."

"A lion is a cat as big as Brownie. Slippy says it has a mane like Brownie's too."

The barn was quiet. The few horses that were still indoors didn't move.

"You know, Slippy can make a mountain out of a molehill," I said.

"Yeah."

I thought about what Shorty had said last night: "I think he's worried. His leg hurt more today, and he said it felt hot. When Jane unwrapped it, she seemed surprised by what it looked like. It smelled funny too. Jane didn't say much, but Kaiser and I could tell something was wrong."

I couldn't think of anything to say that would make Kaiser feel better, so I ate my hay and waited.

The barn was still quiet when Jane came to treat Kaiser's leg. She tended to his wound, gave him his antibiotic injection, and left without saying much. It was almost noon before Kaiser spoke again.

"My leg's infected."

"What?" I didn't know Kaiser could whisper, but I could barely hear him.

"My leg is infected." A little louder, but not much.

I wanted to ask if Jane had talked about the zoo but the thought of Brownie with cat fangs popped into my head. Nothing I could think of seemed right. *It's been quiet too long, say something.*

"Does it hurt a lot?" What a stupid question—of course it hurts.

"It hurt more yesterday, but it's still hot and throbbing."

"If it hurts less today, maybe that's a good sign."

"And maybe it's not." Kaiser was whispering again. "The vet was here last night and things aren't looking good. Jane cried a little. I've never seen Jane cry."

Chapter 19

Kaiser Is Back

Everyone had questions and comments when Kaiser was back in the field with us. "How are you doing? Does it still hurt? Those scars sure are ugly. How did you like being in a box stall all this time?"

Kaiser seemed to enjoy the attention. "It's not as bad as it looks. It still hurts sometimes, but I don't limp at all when I trot." He demonstrated that fact, talking as he circled us. "I think I handled this pretty well."

In the light of day, the scars looked like a snake made of calloused rawhide had wrapped itself around his leg. The wound had become infected twice, and Jane had called the vet several times but she never called the zoo. By the time the bandages could be removed, the wound had healed over but it had a raised ridge of flesh with an angry red glow. That glow faded to dried rope that looked like it would crack and bleed if he moved, but Jane kept it clean and slathered in a thick coating of salve. The snake of a scar flexed as he trotted around his friends.

"I'd rather pick up saddles than lose you," Jane spoke to Kaiser when she poured his scoop of grain that afternoon.

I was sandwiched between Kaiser and Shorty again, and that night, when the barn lights were turned off: *Thump.*

"Are you kidding me?" Shorty asked.

Thump.

"A guy has to do what a guy has to do," Kaiser responded.

Thump.

"Oh, dear me," Shorty said.

"I injured my left rear, but this job requires my right."

Thump.

A saddle fell beyond the tack room wall and we all laughed.

Chapter 20

Circles

"What are you doing?" I asked Smokey as he walked in a little circle around a gnarled apple tree. I'd watched him doing this last fall, but I had been new to the herd and didn't want to pry. Smokey hadn't done it all winter, but with the snow gone he was circling again.

"It's an old habit, and old habits die hard," he said. I could see a circular rut around several trees nearby.

"How did you get into this habit?" I couldn't understand why he would walk around and around and around.

"I traveled with a carnival for a few years after I left the rodeo," Smokey said. "I walked in a circle with five other horses. Well, I was the only horse, the rest were ponies. People paid to put their children on our backs and we walked them in a circle. It didn't make sense to me, but people kept paying and we kept walking."

"But you don't have to do that anymore."

"It's soothing. I know it sounds silly, but I find the act of walking in circles relaxing."

He must have liked doing pony rides. I loved what I used to do. I'd worked in big circles in the flat classes; walk, trot, canter left, then walk, trot, and canter right. We were always in the ribbons. Nancy said it was because I was a great mover, smooth as silk.

I got to jump over fences in the other classes and I loved it; it felt like I was flying.

Kaiser walked toward us and Smokey stepped away from the tree and started to graze. I guessed he was through with relaxing for a while.

Kaiser and I walked up the hill, where some of the hay from this morning was still on the ground. We ate and talked, and in a few moments I saw Smokey walking around his tree again. Watching him was oddly calming. I wondered if Smokey felt younger when he walked around trees. If walking in circles could make me feel like a show horse again, I would do it all day long.

"Don't start walking around trees, Big Guy, or you'll never stop. I've seen it too many times." Kaiser placed his body between me and Smokey's tree.

I didn't need to see Smokey to imagine another course of fences. This one would be even higher, so I could fly again.

Chapter 21

Slippy Gets Caught

"What's going on?" I asked.

Slippy was leaning on the new wooden fence that had replaced the wire he'd pushed his way through a few months before.

"He'll never push through that. Those boards are brand new." Kaiser was back in the school string, being used for lessons, and you'd never guess he'd nearly lost a hoof—unless you looked at the scar.

"Slippy, you can't push your big body through a solid wood fence—"

A snapping sound cut Kaiser short.

The top rail bowed. Slippy gave another push and it snapped again. The two bottom rails remained solid, but the top rail, still attached to the fence posts on either side, had an open gap framed by the ragged edges of broken wood. Slippy stepped over the bottom rails with his front feet.

"I don't believe it," Kaiser said. "All he has to do now is step over with his back legs and we're all free. You are a wonder, Slippy."

I worried that Shorty and Brownie would be too short to step over the bottom rails. It would be easy for me, but I didn't want to leave them behind. "Shorty, you can't step over that."

"I can jump it." Shorty was ready.

"Me too," Brownie said.

Were they thinking about how much fun it would be to trot down the lane and then gallop like wild horses when we got to the road? I had only felt that freedom once, and I couldn't wait to do it again.

Slippy walked forward, but before his hind legs reached the lower rails he stopped. The top rail was broken but still

attached to the posts on either side, and when Slippy's hips got to that board, it didn't open wide enough. We waited but he didn't move. He adjusted himself, bending his knees to pull himself forward, pushing with his hind legs. The board creaked where the nails held to the posts, but the opening did not widen.

"Slippy, you've stopped yourself," Shorty said. "You're going to have to come right back in here with the rest of us."

"I don't give up that easy, little lady." Slippy gave a heave and gained an inch. He adjusted his stance and gave another try, but could not move forward. "I'm not done yet." He grunted and gained nothing, groaned but didn't move at all.

"All right, you've proven you're tough and can push through a new fence rail, now give up and get back in here," Shorty said.

Slippy didn't move. I waited for him to shove his way through. He readjusted his feet a few times, but made no forward motion. He took a half-step back and stopped.

"We're getting bored." Kaiser turned to walk away. "I told you that you wouldn't be able to push through a brand new fence. Just back up and admit you're not as strong as you thought you were."

"I can't," Slippy said. "When I try to back up the edges of the broken board poke into my sides." Slippy looked around to examine his predicament. "I'm stuck."

Kaiser spun around. "What do you mean, stuck?"

I could see the problem. Slippy's shoulders and ribcage were through the opening left by the broken rail, but his hips wouldn't fit. When he backed up, the jagged edges of the board poked him in the ribs. There was blood and hair stuck to the broken board that would not let him pass.

"Be careful, Slippy, you're bleeding," I said.

"Come on, big boy, you can do this. Push on through there." Kaiser had a funny way of trying to help.

I moved up beside Slippy as much as I could. "If I push on the rail, will it help?"

"You could try, but I don't think it'll work. You'll only be able to push with your head and neck. You can't fit in here with me."

I set my forehead against the rail, but it didn't move.

"Nothing moved," Slippy announced.

"Kaiser, why don't you get on the other side and give that rail a shove. If we both push, it might work."

Kaiser moved up and set his face against the rail. "I'm ready, Big Guy, let's give it a try."

"Nothing."

Shorty pushed in next to me. "Let's give it another try. My neck may be short, but it's strong."

Four horse rumps bunched together.

"Okay, Big Guy, you say the word and we'll all push." I couldn't believe Kaiser made me the leader. I was in charge.

"Now!"

We all gave it our best.

"Nothing." Slippy sounded disappointed.

A whistle peeled from the barnyard gate and the other horses started to move toward their afternoon grain. Brownie looked back. "Grain time."

Kaiser, Shorty, and I stayed with Slippy.

Another whistle called. "You guys go ahead. Jane will come and get me."

"Are you sure?" I asked. "Don't try to back up any more, you'll hurt yourself."

"You don't want to go through that kind of injury," Kaiser said. "It took me months before I could walk right. Just wait here, Jane will come looking for you." He was trotting toward the gate.

"Don't worry, Slippy, she'll take care of this." Shorty was trotting too.

I hung back.

"Go ahead, Big Guy, Jane will come and get me. I'm not sure what she can do, but she'll figure out something."

I hesitated.

"Go on, Big Guy, the quicker you get back to the barn, the sooner she'll come and find me."

I cantered to catch up with Shorty and Kaiser. We were the last horses in the barn, and everyone was eating the grain and hay that had been waiting in their stalls. Jane snapped our halters to the ropes in the front of the stalls and latched the chains behind us.

"All right, what have you done with Slippy?" She held the hook from his rump chain in the air. "Kaiser, Shorty, Big Guy—did your little gang have something to do with this?"

We're not a gang, we're a herd. I'm part of a herd and we almost went for a wild run. I hope Jane goes out to get Slippy now.

I could hear Jane's half of the conversation as she spoke on the phone hanging on the wall near the tack room.

"Ben, can you bring a chainsaw from the house? Slippy has gotten himself stuck in the new three-board fence.

"Yeah, he broke the top rail.

"The bottom two rails are fine.

"I tried that, I can't get the nails out.

"Bring a crowbar if you want, but I think you're going to need a chainsaw."

We could hear the chainsaw roar to life, and Slippy was in the barn a few minutes later. "You are in some big trouble, Slivovitz. Ben just put that fence in last week. I should leave these wounds on your sides untreated, to teach you a lesson."

Jane secured Slippy in his stall and stomped out of the barn.

"Does it hurt much?" Kaiser asked.

"They're just scrapes. I didn't push that hard once I knew I was stuck."

"Will they be okay if Jane doesn't treat them?" I asked.

"She'll be back," Shorty said.

"I know I'm in trouble when she calls me Slivovitz. Maybe she won't . . ."

Soon, Jane entered Slippy's stall with a bucket of water, a bottle of soap, and a jar of salve.

"That's the stuff she treated me with. It really works," Kaiser whispered.

"Slippy, what are we going to do with you?" Jane asked. "This is almost as bad as the night you led this motley crew into the Dowsborough Woods. These wounds aren't bad, you'll be in lessons this afternoon, but I'm wondering how we can keep you in the pasture. Why do you have to break through every fence?"

Chapter 22

THE DOWSBOROUGH WOODS

Jane was out of the barn when I asked, "What happened in the Dowsborough Woods?"

"That was two years ago, before you were here, Big Guy," Shorty said. "Slippy, you should tell the story."

Slippy coughed, cleared his throat, and began. "It was a lovely summer night. Fireflies were—"

"Just tell the story, Slippy, don't get all fancy with it," Kaiser said.

"Let him tell his story," Shorty said.

"It was a lovely summer night. Fireflies were flickering all over the pasture. The fence on that side of the pasture was easy to break through. The wire was old and patched, re-patched, then patched again. I knew it was too dark to gallop down the road, and definitely too dark to canter through the woods, but there was a garden out there. I'd discovered it on an earlier outing. The cabin at the end of the lane had a cleared area for a garden, and there is always good eating in a garden.

"We'd browsed the vegetables, eaten fruit under the apple trees, and grazed the lawn when I spotted hostas under the only window with a light on. There was a humming woman in there washing things in a pan of water under the window. They clattered now and then, and she hummed a little louder. It seemed rude not to say hello, but she didn't notice me when I stood right outside the window. I thought that if I put my head where she could see it, she might give me a scratch on the neck or, even better, more treats from the house.

"My head was over her pan of water before I realized there was a screen in the window. It was easy to push through, but the lady's scream frightened me. I pulled my head back, taking the frame of the screen with me. The wire mesh held the wooden frame in place like a clown collar. I had worn a clown collar back when I was with the circus. Little kids thought it was cute.

"The woman was yelling to other people in the house, so I thought we should get out of there. Lights were turning on everywhere when we cantered into the woods.

"The next morning, I was still wearing my window-screen collar when Jane called us in from the field for breakfast. I remember her words, 'Slippy, Slippy, Slippy.

What did you get into last night?'

"I heard all about what it cost to replace the screen, and the garden, and the lawn, and the new fence that Ben put up.

"That new wire fence went up the next day and two years later I still haven't found a weak spot anywhere. It's the toughest fence I've ever seen."

"I wish I'd been here for that escape," I said.

"There will be more, Big Guy. Many more." Slippy bobbed his head as he spoke.

Chapter 23

Coyotes

I was wide awake and not sure why. There was something out there but I couldn't see it. I was trying to hear it again, smell it, sense its movement. There it went, slinking beyond Paper Moon's sleeping body.

Then I was standing, unsure how I got up so fast. I heard other horses moving as I raced toward a dark figure. The figure lifted its head, eyes glowing, ears erect. The coyote turned to run and I followed. Yellow Dog was beside me with Kaiser behind him. There were five coyotes racing away from us.

I slowed down,

thinking they were far enough away, and Yellow Dog did the same. Kaiser raced past us. "I'll chase them to the fence line. I'd chase them further if I could."

The herd was milling around, half-awake.

"Are you all right?" Yellow Dog nuzzled Paper Moon's neck.

"I'm fine." She shook her head.

"How about you?" He looked at Smokey.

"Yeah, yeah, I'm okay."

Slippy stood next to Smokey. "He's all right."

"I already said that." Smokey huffed.

Noble Road and Star Shadow stood together. The top of Shadow's shoulder was half-way up Noble's shoulder blade. Shorty called them the long and short of it. The mismatched pair were always together.

Shorty moved up next to me, and we both looked into the distance. "Where's Kaiser?" she asked.

"He said he was going to chase them to the fence line, but I wanted to come back and make sure there weren't more of them back here," I said.

"Coyotes usually stay together, but I'm glad you came back to tell us what's going on," Shorty said. "I wish Kaiser would come back. I don't like him being out there alone."

I looked around to make sure our herd was all here. "I don't like Kaiser being out there either."

"I'm just fine." Kaiser was trotting toward us. "You should have seen those dogs clambering and crawling over and under the fence. They couldn't get out of here fast enough. I made sure they knew there'd be trouble if they came back."

Kaiser walked through the herd calling out names to

make sure they knew he was counting them. "Paper Moon, Yellow Dog, Smokey, Noble Road, Slivovitch, Star Sha—"

"We're all here," Slippy said.

"It's a good thing I woke up and ran them off." Kaiser was strutting.

"Big Guy was the first one awake," Yellow Dog said. "You were still stumbling around, half-awake."

"I'm the one who ran them to the fence line to get rid of them." Kaiser's strut didn't change.

"Yes," Shorty said. "I was worried about you."

"Coyotes don't prey on something as big as a horse unless it's hurt or weak. They go after things like rabbits and squirrels." Kaiser's strut was more distinct.

He's got to be the hero, I thought.

"Thanks, Kaiser, for getting the coyotes out of here."

"No troubles, glad to do it," he replied. The arch in his neck grew an inch.

BIG GUY'S SECOND SCHOOL HORSE YEAR

Chapter 24

The Zoo?!

"What's going on, Kaiser?" I asked as soon as I was back in my stall.

"Yeah, why did Jane pull you from the lesson and replace you with Big Guy?" Shorty and I had been passing questioning looks back and forth during a simple walk, trot, canter lesson, but we hadn't had the chance to talk.

"My leg's a little stiff," Kaiser said. "I was going to work it out but Jane stopped me before I could get warmed up."

"I've noticed you limping a little bit when we go out in the morning," Shorty said. "But by the time we're out in the field you seem to be fine and I forget to ask about it."

"Aren't we all a little stiff in the morning? We aren't exactly spring chickens." Kaiser gave his bum leg a stomp. "It feels fine now. I just needed a few more minutes to warm up."

I knew I shouldn't say it, but I did. "This is the third time this week Jane pulled you out of a lesson, and she hasn't used you in a jumping lesson in weeks."

"Are you concerned about me or complaining because you're getting more of the little-kid jumping lessons now?"

"I'm worried about you," I said. "Okay, the little-kid riders feel like a balancing act sometimes. Most of them are pretty good but when they get a little behind at a fence they can be scary. I worry they might topple right off, but they hang on."

I wondered how the older school horses had been doing this for years. Have they ever had a balanced, confident rider on their back? I'm learning how difficult this job can be. At first I only got the advanced riders, but now I'm being used more for intermediate riders.

We stopped talking when we heard Jane making a call from the phone on the wall near the tack room. We like to listen in when she talks on the phone.

"Hello, Jersey?

"Yeah, I have a question about Kaiser.

"I know, you warned me.

"He seems okay most of the time but I'm worried about what's going to happen in the winter. The cold weather will probably make it worse.

"I've had to pull him from lessons and I can't afford to keep a pasture ornament. If I kept every horse I wanted but could no longer use, I'd have twenty-five horses and no money to feed them.

"I've been putting off that call but I can see it coming, and I shouldn't wait any longer.

"I guess you have to come out and look him over first. You're out here Monday for fall vaccinations, can you do it then?

"Great, I'll make the call tonight.

"I know, I know. It's just so hard to do. I like that old stinker.

"See you Monday."

We heard the receiver click into place and Jane going into the tack room.

I said what we were all thinking: "Is she going to call the zoo?"

No one answered.

Chapter 25

Little Lisa's Lesson

Jane came out of the tack room with bridles hanging along the length of both arms. She hung a bridle on the hook next to each school horse's stall. On weekends the lessons go all day, and she gets the tack ready early. She hung my bridle last, then walked back into the tack room, leaving Kaiser's bridle hook empty.

Kaiser glanced around as Jane walked past his stall. *I should say something encouraging, but I can't think straight.*

"Looks like you get another day off," I said. *That was stupid, another day off because he's lame, another day off before he goes to the zoo. Why didn't I just keep my mouth shut?*

Little Lisa ducked under the chain behind my stall and climbed onto the wooden deck that I eat my hay and grain from. She groomed my face, as she had in the past. She brushed the area under my jaw and my lip twitched.

She wriggled her tiny body to the floor and groomed up as high as she could reach. My legs were well groomed and my stomach and lower chest spotless. Little Lisa has grown since I became a school horse. I can't believe it's been a year since I arrived in the School Horse barn and first met this little child.

She was climbing back onto my feed rack when Kaiser said, "Don't let her hug your face, Big Guy. If you let children hug your head you'll become one of the popular horses and never get a moment's rest."

Lisa was at eye level on the feed rack. "I'm seven years old and I can take lessons now." She was combing the hair in my forelock. "Jane said I could ride you today."

What, how can Jane put this baby on my back? She's so little and she doesn't know anything. What if my trot is too fast or too bouncy? What if she pulls on the reins to get her balance? This is a very bad idea.

I'd been downgraded to intermediate and advanced riders, but I had never been used in a novice or beginner lesson.

Jane came in to finish my grooming. "This is going to be a new one for both of us, Big Guy."

I thought I heard Kaiser chuckling.

Jane slipped the bridle over my head. "Little Lisa really wants to ride you, and Shorty has been very busy with Kaiser out of action. I hope you're up for this," she said to me.

Jane allowed Little Lisa to lead me into the indoor ring, but she walked with us. Lisa was so short, I had to dip my head to see her. *Should I put my head down to make it easier for her to lead me?* I thought. *If I did that, would she try to hug me?*

Lisa managed to get into the saddle from the mounting

block, but she had to stretch the way most people do to mount from the ground. Her little legs rested on the saddle skirt, the part of the saddle that hangs down my body. Her legs didn't touch me at all. *How could she ride with such short legs?*

"I see that you already know how to hold the reins," Jane said.

"I've been watching for a long time." Lisa patted my neck. "This is the most fun day of my life."

"Nudge with your legs to get him to walk." Jane held the lead line. I could hardly feel the motion of Lisa's legs, but I walked when Jane did.

"Pull back to make him stop," Jane said. I stopped, although Lisa's gesture barely touched my mouth.

"Make him walk again." I felt a whisper of movement and began to walk.

A light touch and I moved left, then right as Lisa learned to walk, turn both ways, and stop.

Some intermediate riders were less subtle with their hands. They didn't hurt me when they turned or stopped, but they applied more pressure than necessary. Little Lisa had light hands. She really had been paying attention.

At the end of the lesson we trotted around the ring with Jane jogging next to us. I tried to take little steps so I wouldn't bounce Lisa too much. Her seat stayed in the saddle, her hips so relaxed she didn't bounce at all. *Lisa is going to be a wonderful, sensitive horsewoman*, I thought. I imagined her winning blue ribbons at Madison Square Garden. *Is this how Shorty feels about her young students?*

Jane stood back and followed Lisa and me back into the barn. I lowered my head so she didn't have to reach up so high, and Lisa put the reins in her left hand and rested her right hand behind my ears to give them a scratch. She knew I loved that.

Kaiser was laughing after they walked away. *How can he be jolly when he knows what's going to happen to him on Monday?* If he wasn't going to let the call to the zoo bother him, I'd pretend not to worry too.

"She didn't hug my head," I told him.

"Not yet, but I can see it coming," he said.

Chapter 26

Kaiser's Trailer Arrives

The vet backed Kaiser out of his stall. I was glad I could see what they were doing with my old friend. Jane held his lead rope while Dr. Loewith checked Kaiser's heart and lungs. He looked at his eyes with that bright light. I hate when they do that. The vet held Kaiser's tongue to one side and checked his teeth, then moved his tongue to the other side. *It feels so strange to have your tongue pulled from side to side like that.* The vet rolled up his stethoscope and put it in his pocket.

"You've had regular exams and vaccines, so we don't have to worry about much. I can certify him good to go," said the vet.

"Thanks, I was sure he would be all right, except for occasional lameness, and I suppose they don't care about that where he's going," Jane said.

Jane led Kaiser back to his stall and patted him on the neck. "They'll be picking you up this afternoon. Sorry I can't keep you buddy, but this is the best I can do for you," she told Kaiser.

Hay munching had stopped. All the horses were listening. The click of Jane's bootheels on the concrete sounded like a horse walking away. *How could she be so casual about sending Kaiser to the zoo?*

I heard a truck and trailer pull into the parking area. *This is it. Kaiser is leaving and we all know where he's going.* A man walked into the barn wearing black pants and a white shirt with the sleeves rolled up. His tie was loose, the way many of the fathers looked when they came to pick up their children. He ducked under Kaiser's rump chain.

"I can't believe you're in the same stall. Do you remember me? I'm Jeff. I rode you when I was a kid. I used to dream about owning you," he said.

It's one of Kaiser's old students coming to say goodbye. I wonder how he knew what was going to happen. He doesn't seem sad— why did he come?

"I have a little girl named Ellie," this Jeff guy continued. "She has a pony, but Buttercup needs a stablemate. I'm told you can't work too hard but you should still get a little exercise. How would you like this old guy to ride you around while he teaches his daughter how to ride? We'll only do as much as your leg will allow," he continued.

Shorty whispered, "He's going to take Kaiser home with him!"

Jeff was patting Kaiser's neck. "Mostly you'll be in a pasture with a little palomino pony and plenty of grass with a little clover. I hope you like clover."

You mean I'm going to be babysitting a little yellow pony?

Kaiser didn't say it but I could guess his thoughts.

Jeff took Kaiser's old halter off and slipped on a supple leather halter with a shiny nameplate. "I couldn't fit your whole name on this halter. 'I Was Kaiser Bill's Batman' is way too long," he said. "I hope you don't mind that I just put Batman on it. Ellie loves Batman, but I'll always call you Kaiser."

Kaiser had been so funny about his name and made fun of other horse's names, I wondered how he was going to feel about being called Batman.

"Come on, old buddy, let's go home." They were walking down the barn aisle when Jeff said, "Do you remember when I used to sing Rhinestone Cowboy during riding lessons? Ellie giggles when I sing that song while she rides Buttercup."

The silence lasted long after the trailer drove off. I was happy for Kaiser, but part of me wanted to go with my old friend. If I did, I would leave Shorty, Slippy, and Yellow Dog. Today was a whirlwind of emotions; was I happy or sad? I wondered what Shorty was thinking, but needed to wait a while before I asked her.

No one talked much that night.

Chapter 27

A New School Horse

A few days after Kaiser left, we came in for our afternoon grain to find a buckskin mare standing in Kaiser's old stall. She was taller than Kaiser and her dingy yellow coat stood out against her black mane and tail. I didn't like seeing another horse in Kaiser's stall.

"Hi, I'm Shorty. What's your name?" *We can count on Shorty to get things started.*

"Bucky," she replied.

I knew Kaiser would have had something to say about a buckskin horse named Bucky. I could almost hear his voice: *What an original name, almost like naming you Horsie. You must have another name.* I asked the question for him. "Do you have a registered name?"

"Buttercup." I almost fell over. Kaiser was living at Jeff's house with a pony named Buttercup! "I'm mostly quarter horse, but I'm not registered," she added.

Bucky told her story of being a backyard horse, belonging

to a family with four children. She was going to miss them but she said she wouldn't be here long. The family was going away for the winter and they would come back for her in the spring.

"Don't believe that story," Yellow Dog said.

I realized he and Bucky were almost the same color, but Yellow Dog's white mane and tail made him look brighter than Bucky, not dingy at all.

"My people walked away from me without saying a word," Yellow Dog said. "Jane told me they were going to Japan, wherever that is, and they'd be back in the fall. That was two years ago," he said.

"This place looks pretty good to me," Bucky said. "I'll miss my box stall, but the grain and hay here are fresh and the stalls are clean and well-bedded. I used to be on a rent-a-horse string," she continued. "People came and paid to ride for an hour. Most of them didn't know anything about horses, and sometimes they were pretty rough. But usually they were scared. We would walk around and eat grass and they couldn't figure out how to make us behave. I almost felt guilty. The stalls weren't very clean, the hay was sometimes moldy, and the grain was so dusty it made me cough. I think they bought the cheapest feed they could get.

"But that's where I met the Parkers. They were on vacation when they came to ride one day, then they came back to ride again. It was fun to carry the youngest Parker child, Janet, around—she knew how to ride. She told me she would take me home if she could. A few days later, they came with a trailer and I went home with them. I've been there for more than four years." She hesitated. "I'll miss getting Christmas carrots this year."

I watched Bucky's face soften, focusing on a memory.

Yellow Dog grunted.

"Jane gives us apples on Christmas morning," I said. "She makes apple pies and we get the peels and cores and extra apples when she's done."

"That's in the morning," Shorty said. "On Christmas afternoon she drops big red-and-white hard candy mints on top of our grain," she added.

Shorty took the conversation over to explain how the lesson and turnout program worked around here, while I thought about the mints Nancy used to give me.

Chapter 28

BUCKY'S BIG ESCAPE

Clink—the chain and hook that held the gate closed rang as it fell against the metal gate.

Bucky had become friends with Paper Moon, Smokey, and Yellow Dog. Yellow Dog told me that Bucky said she could open almost every gate latch she'd ever seen. When I asked her about it she seemed shy, but then admitted she could use her lips and tongue to unsnap most hooks. I told her Slippy used to push his big body through weak fencing and lead us on wild excursions, but the new fencing seemed to be Slippy-proof.

Bucky wriggled her nose around the gate hook, took it in her mouth, and shook it a bit. It took a long time, and I thought she may have been bragging about a skill she didn't possess, but then the chain dropped and she pushed the gate open.

She stood back and nodded to Slippy, "I don't know this area, you should take the lead," Bucky said.

Slippy hesitated, then walked through the gate with his herd behind him. The skeleton crew that worked Mondays, when the farm was closed, had left after morning chores. They wouldn't be back until the afternoon feeding, so we were in the clear.

My friend Ding was in a paddock behind the border barn, and I stopped to see him. I missed talking to my show horse friends. Bucky was near the back of the herd, and she walked over. "Do you want him to come with us?"

"What are you talking about?" Ding was looking at me.

"We're going for a wild run," I said. "You'd love it."

"I don't know about that." Ding took a step back.

"I do," said Taylor Maid in the next paddock. "Can I go too? Come on, Ding, we'll have a good time."

"Can you do this?" I asked Bucky.

She had Ding's gate open with a couple of wriggles of her lips.

"That's how it usually works," she said. She pushed the gate open, but Ding stepped back again.

Bucky had Taylor Maid's gate open even faster. Taylor Maid pushed the gate wide, bumping it into Bucky, who couldn't get out of the way fast enough. Taylor Maid was ready to go.

"Come on, Ding," she said. "This is going to be great, what are you afraid of?"

"I'm not afraid." Ding didn't move.

"We've done it before," I reassured him. "It's kind of wild, and so much fun."

Ding stepped through the gate. Bucky looked around.

"What are you looking for?" I asked.

"Is there anyone else you want to let out?" The other paddocks were empty.

"Not unless you can open stall doors this easily," I said.

"I haven't been able to master that one," she admitted.

The four of us trotted to catch up with the rest of the herd.

On the road we cantered, then galloped in a wild rush. Ding and Taylor Maid stayed near me. They seemed to be afraid of the school horses. Ding relaxed into a steady snort as he galloped, and I could tell he was enjoying the run.

"Isn't this great?" Taylor Maid shouted over the sound of hooves pounding the gravel road.

Ding gave a big snort and I did the same. We were wild horses on the move.

I thought we were going back to the swimming pool yard, but we turned onto a road before we got there. We passed a house and raced into a freshly mown field. We galloped to the middle of a huge flat pasture and Slippy spun around, bringing his herd to a halt.

"I knew this was a hay field but I didn't know it had just been cut. This is perfect." He strutted a circle around us. "Enjoy, enjoy.'"

The fragrance of fresh cut hay filled the air, and we grazed the richest pasture I had ever tasted.

"Isn't this better than standing in a dirt paddock all afternoon?" Taylor Maid nudged Ding. He was too busy eating to answer.

I didn't want to like Kaiser's replacement, but Bucky was alright. She was grazing next to Smokey and Paper Moon like she'd been part of our herd for years.'

"There they are." A truck had stopped on the road. Our two-man Monday crew approached with lead ropes in hand. "Come on, you nags, the party's over."

"We should run," Ding said.

I was about to agree when Brownie spoke up. "No, no, no. Never run. Why waste all that energy?"

"Ponies are always in favor of saving their energy," Slippy said.

"That's why we live so long. Watch and learn." Brownie stepped between us and the approaching men.

Jesse, the younger of the two wranglers, got to Brownie first. With the lead rope in his right hand, his left hand was about to touch Brownie's halter. I thought Brownie had miscalculated, but he turned his head and took three steps. Jesse stopped, moved over with his left hand out again, and Brownie slowly turned his rump to that hand and trotted toward us.

"That's how you do it. Let them think you're going to just stand there, and then move as little as possible. Don't trot, canter, or gallop. A few steps is all it takes," he said.

We walked away when they tried to get near us. Each horse understood the plan, and not one of us trotted or ran away. I thought it was an ingenious method.

The elder Monday-man approached Ding. My old friend tipped his nose toward the extended hand, I thought he was about to surrender, then Ding turned his head and took four steps.

"This is as much fun as charging down the road," Ding whispered. "I don't like that old guy. The young one's not so bad, but that old guy doesn't like horses." Ding was as relaxed as I'd ever seen him.

Old Monday-man almost caught Ding again. The snap on the lead rope was inches from connecting to the ring on Ding's halter when he lifted his head and took two steps back. The man balled up the rope and threw it at Ding's chest. Our herd reacted as one, and raced to the far side of the field.

The truck sped off in a cloud of dust.

The sun was low in the sky when the truck stopped in the same place and three people got out. The men had brought Jane with them. The two men began marching toward us, but Jane said, "You wait here, let me see what I can do."

"Yeah, right." The old guy folded his arms across his chest, letting the lead rope hang from his hand. "You think a little girl can catch this pack of nags?"

"She thinks cuz' she's a riding instructor, she knows it all," the younger Monday-man said under his breath, but we still heard it.

I thought Jane would catch Shorty, as she had in the past, but instead she walked up to me. "Hey, Big Guy, have you had a pleasant afternoon? This field smells good enough to eat. How about we gather up your herd and take them home for some grain?"

She led me back to the men.

Why did she say this was my herd? I thought.

"Could I have another lead rope, please. I'll use them as reins so I can ride this guy back; the herd will follow him. I think he's becoming their leader."

I'm not their leader, Slippy brought us here. Why would she think I'm the leader?

"Jesse, could you give me a leg up?" Jane bent her left knee, then she was on my back, light as a feather.

"You guys can wait here," Jane said. "I think they'll follow me and you can bring up the rear with the truck. Once you're in the driveway, stop and close the gates near the road," she told the crew.

I looked back at the field and all the horses were looking at me. Ding and Taylor Maid stood halfway between me and the herd.

"The school horses should follow me right into the barn and into their stalls," Jane said. "But I'm not sure what Ding and Taylor Maid will do. This is a new one for me," she admitted.

"You think they're just going to follow you, like a row of little ducks?" Old Monday-man's arms had unfolded.

"No, I think they're going to follow me like a herd of wild horses. They are horses, after all."

"We'll see." Old Monday-man and Jesse walked toward the truck, the old guy shaking his head.

Jane and I strolled back to the herd with Ding and Taylor Maid behind us. "These two might actually follow us like a pair of little ducks." Jane was looking back at them, laughing.

We were halfway around the herd, and they were grazing again. We started to trot and Jane rode through the group and cued me to canter. We moved toward the truck as a cantering herd. I thought we would go behind the truck and turn left, but Jane guided me in a wide arc in front of the truck, and as we passed the open driver's-side window she made a funny noise, "Quack, quack."

Back in our stalls, still buzzing with the excitement of the afternoon, I heard Jane on the phone. "I don't know, all the gates were open," she said. "Yeah, I'm thinking some smart aleck kid thought this would be fun."

"And it was," Bucky whispered.

I thought about the herd following me back. Did I *let* Slippy lead us up the road? *I wonder what would happen if I said we should go another way? Would they follow me instead?*

Chapter 29

YELLOW DOG'S PERSON

"You don't remember me, do you?" A stranger was patting Yellow Dog's neck.

I'd watched her walk across the pasture like she knew where she was going. She looked like many of the moms who dropped children off for lessons, but I didn't recognize her and didn't understand why she was crying.

"It's me, Emma Sanders, Justin and Jimmy's mom. It's been so long you've probably forgotten all about us. But we didn't forget you. Justin still has your picture on his corkboard. Jim's job went crazy and we're living between France and Japan now," she said.

This is the woman who promised to come back for Yellow Dog, I thought. *The one he's been so angry with. She looks like a nice lady. Nancy was nice, too, and she cried when she sent me to the school horse barn. Now she walks through the barn with her new horse almost every day and doesn't even notice me.*

"You look great," Emma said. "I knew Jane would take

good care of you." She straightened Yellow Dog's mane. "I would keep your mane a little shorter, but it's clean and combed, and you look well-fed and sassy."

Yellow Dog looked stunned. How would I feel if Nancy talked to me like this?

"We've thought about getting you to Japan, but it would cost so much and I've heard horror stories about horses getting sick or dying during transport. I couldn't take that chance." Yellow Dog nuzzled her hand.

"Now you remember me." She reached in her pocket, pulled out an apple, and held it out to him. "You're the only horse I ever heard of who eats an apple like a person, one little bite at a time." She was crying as apple juice dribbled off her hand.

She talked for a long time and fed Yellow Dog two big apples. She was laughing when she gave him a final pat and said, "Well, I have to go, old buddy. I'd like to think I'll

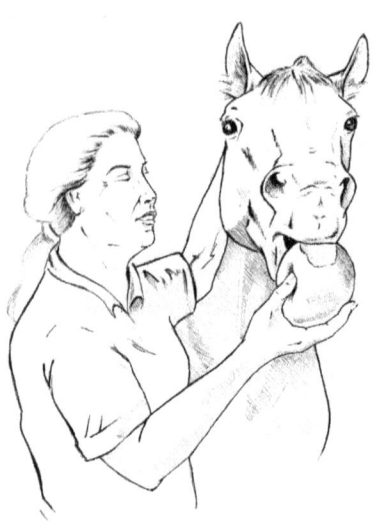

be back soon but I just don't know. It's good to see you looking healthy and happy." She pulled a camera from her other pocket and took a picture of Yellow Dog. "I have to show the boys how great you look."

Yellow Dog followed her back to the gate and stood there long after she left.

I trotted up to him. "Are you all right?" I didn't want to leave him there by himself.

"Yeah. Emma used to be my person. I don't think she's ever coming back though."

"You didn't think she'd be here today." Shorty had walked up behind me.

"This goodbye sounded final," Yellow Dog said. "She told me she gets letters from Jane. Jane sent Emma a picture of me with that goofy frog costume I had to wear during the Halloween class last year."

"It sounds like they still care about you," Shorty said.

The three of us stood at the gate and I tried to think of something to say that wasn't stupid. Yellow Dog turned and looked across the pasture. "I guess this is a nice place to live."

"You've got friends like us," Shorty said.

"It could be worse, couldn't it?" He gave her a nudge with his shoulder and flicked a hind hoof at me.

We'd been grazing for a while and I looked around at the rolling pasture full of healthy, round horses and recalled Bucky's comment: "This place looks pretty good to me."

Nancy put me in a place where she knew I would get good care. My school horse workload was light, the feed was good, and I was part of a herd for the first time since I was a foal. I could hear Kaiser's words in the air: "This is the way horses are supposed to live, outside and moving around all day. The way nature intended."

I missed him more than I missed Nancy.

Chapter 30

Missing Kaiser

Why would I miss Kaiser more than Nancy? I'd only known him for a year and a half, but I had known her much longer. Nancy and I had shown all over the country, winning ribbons and trophies everywhere. We had qualified for the national finals at Madison Square Garden every year—but I now missed Kaiser more, and I wasn't sure why.

"Because you're both horses and Nancy's not," Shorty said.

"I didn't realize anyone was close enough to hear me talking to myself," I said. *This is embarrassing*, I thought. "I was thinking about Yellow Dog's person," I said. *But now I'm thinking about Nancy and how she and I connected when we were competing. Sometimes I could almost hear her thoughts and I wondered if she could hear mine. But I can't say that to Shorty, she wouldn't understand. She's been a school horse most of her life. She's never had a person who worked with her for years. She's never felt that connection with one human.*

"Yellow Dog's person seems to really care about him," I said. "Like that student who came back for Kaiser when he went lame—what was his name?"

"Jeff. His name was Jeff," Shorty said. "I was relieved when Kaiser got to go live with him. I'm sure Jeff will take care of Kaiser for the rest of his life."

"What if something like that happened to us? If we went lame—or worse?" I asked.

"I've been around for a long time . . ." Shorty said. "I'll tell you about Fury. He was a good school horse and he jumped well, but I watched him go downhill when he got sick. He had something wrong that made him drink a lot of water, lose weight along his top-line, and develop a big hay-belly. He kept his winter coat all summer long."

"What was wrong with him?" It sounded awful.

"I can't remember—some kind of tumor or something. He said it didn't hurt but I watched his energy fade," Shorty continued.

"The important thing is that Jane adjusted his workload as he got sicker. He went from jumping a lot to just doing cross poles with beginners. Then she just used him on the flat, no jumping, and eventually she used him for walk-trot beginners only. Jane took care of him until it was time for him to leave. I heard her talk about putting him down because he was so sick. He passed away that night, as though he knew it was time."

We both gazed into the distance.

"The point is," Shorty said, "that Jane will take care of us as long as she can, and if she can't, she'll call someone like

Jeff to come and get us. I don't believe she ever would have called the zoo when Kaiser hurt himself. Fury is buried in the far corner of our pasture, along with a few other horses I've known. She didn't call the zoo with any of them."

"But she doesn't own me," I said. "I still belong to Nancy—even though she barely notices me anymore. She paid attention to me for a few days after she got that new horse, What's-His-Name, but that didn't last."

"Jane didn't own Fury either," Shorty said. "He came to be a school horse just like you. Jane still took care of him all his life."

"You're in a good place, Big Guy. Relax and enjoy it." Yellow Dog had been listening.

"And you've got your herd," Bucky said, standing next to Shorty.

"Are you guys sneaking up on me?" I was surprised to see everyone next to me.

Knowing there was an unmarked cemetery in the far corner of the field made that spot special, even sacred. When I was a show horse, I was more connected to my person because I was never turned out with another horse. Nancy was so afraid I might hurt myself, she never allowed me outside with another horse. I'd loved that horse-show life, but I didn't realize how much I should have missed being with other horses.

"This is the way we're supposed to live." I could hear Kaiser's voice in the trees again. I imagined him talking to me often.

"Jane wouldn't call the zoo, ever," Shorty said.

We turned toward Jane's whistle at the pasture gate and

I thought, *I hope Shorty's right.*
　But I said, "I know."

Chapter 31

THE STRANGER

"What was that?" A horse I'd never seen raced past us and disappeared over the hill.

"I don't know," Shorty said. "He seems upset." We could hear him whinny and call as he ran around the back of our pasture.

"What's he doing in our field?" Bucky asked.

"I don't know, but here he comes again." We didn't move as he careened past us, heading back toward the barn. "He's not one of the show horses—I know all of them," I said.

Our herd pulled into a tighter group, waiting to see what the stranger might do next. He was a liver-chestnut. His coat looked like a chestnut that had rolled in mud. He was about fifteen hands, with a stocky build.

"He looks like a quarter horse," Shorty said. "Why is he making all that noise? We quarter horses are usually easygoing."

Shorty was the first quarter horse I'd ever met, and I didn't know anyone more even-tempered. The stranger galloped back to us, trotting back and forth, snorting.

"Hi, I'm Shorty. Who are you?" Shorty's always the first to introduce herself to new horses.

"I'm Champ, short for Champion, and I don't belong out here," he huffed.

I was thinking the same thing. He looked like trouble.

"My person put me out here while she went to lunch and I don't like this at all."

He was prancing back and forth, showing off. "I'm never turned out with other horses. I always have the paddock to myself," he went on.

I remembered how that used to be, back when I was a show horse—kind of lonely.

"This field is nice and big," Shorty said. "There's plenty of room for all of us."

"I don't know about that," he said.

Neither do I. What is this guy's problem? He acts like he wants to take over. The herd stood behind me. Shorty was talking from back there—she was afraid of him, but was still trying to be nice.

The stranger watched me as he paced back and forth, but I couldn't read him. *What is this attitude?* When we didn't respond, he ran back to the gate and did his prancing there, back and forth in front of the gate. When he got tired of that, he began to graze and so did we.

The herd had relaxed and spread out. The stranger was getting closer but no one was paying attention. I wanted to tell them to watch out for this guy, but he was grazing and wandering the way horses usually do. He seemed perfectly normal. Had I misjudged him?

I had relaxed too much, and now the stranger was between me and Paper Moon and Smokey. I should have been paying attention. I'd let him separate two of our weakest horses from the herd. I wanted to get him out of here, but I didn't know how. I grazed and watched, and he was aware of being watched.

A flash of liver against gray, and Smokey screamed. The stranger had his teeth clamped to the base of Smokey's neck. Smokey ran toward me, but the stranger came with him, his front legs across Smokey's back like a human rider, his back legs running beside him to keep up with his prey. Smokey's blood stood out against his nearly-white coat. *Why did I let this happen?*

My ears flat back, mouth open, I slammed into the stranger and we both slid along Smokey's body and slipped off his rump. With the stranger's feet on the ground, he was shorter than I expected. He'd gone after Smokey because he was little and weak.

The stranger's teeth flashed toward my throat, but I brought my front legs up against his chest, and he staggered back a few steps.

"You're picking on the wrong horse, Champ," I said.

"I'm tougher than any horse in this field, and I'm ready to prove it," he roared back.

He was acting like the mustang stallions Kaiser had told

me about. I should have listened more closely to his stories of life on the Montana range, but I never thought I would have to deal with anything like this in the school barn.

The stranger lunged toward me and I reared, striking at his head. I felt my hoof connect with bone. I wasn't sure what part of his head I had hit, but I hit it hard. He staggered, then stood wide-legged, weaving.

"All right, all right, you win. You got me." His legs remained wide, shaking. "I'm sorry I did that—I won't do it again."

"I won't give you the chance." I stretched my body to its full 17.1 hands. The stranger's legs wobbled. He didn't look so tough.

"Look, I'm nervous and I don't want to be here any more than you want me here. Why don't we just leave one another alone? I'll go graze near the gate until my person comes back." He stood straighter, but his legs still trembled.

"Let him go, Big Guy. He'll leave us alone now." Shorty had moved up almost between us, a little more on my side than his. "I think he learned his lesson."

But the stranger charged at Shorty. He was fast, but I cut him off. Crashing my shoulder into his, the strange horse sprawled to the ground, then stayed there—too long. *Did I knock him out?*

He lifted his head and got up slowly. I thought he might pretend to be sorry again but he hurtled toward me. I braced for impact. Hooves and teeth flashed. I felt pain in my right side, and wheeled to kick him. Rump to rump, we kicked one another. *This kicking contest shouldn't last long,* I thought. *My legs are stronger and longer.* I connected solid hits, but most of his glanced off me. I was confident I would win this battle, until Brownie threw himself into the fight.

Brownie, don't do this. You're the only horse out here smaller than this guy. Stay out of it. A kick connected to one of Brownie's front legs. *Was it me or the stranger who kicked him? Is it broken? Does he need help?*

A hoof approached in horrifying slow motion. In the same slow motion, I registered that this horse had shoes on its hind feet. That bright metal shoe, so close to my face.

Why am I on my knees? Why am I thinking about cows? Cows lay down front-legs-first. They go to their knees, rump in the air, then their hind legs fold and they drop to the ground. I was halfway to the ground, cow-style, thinking about cows I hadn't seen since I was a foal, but my hind legs wouldn't fold. I heard the stranger laughing from far away. The sound of my hips hitting the ground didn't make any sense.

Chapter 32

Is He All Right?

"Is he all right?"
"Look at his face."
"Is he breathing?"

I could hear voices from a distance. Shorty, Slippy, Bucky . . . Kaiser. *What's Kaiser doing here?*

I wanted to open my eyes but my head hurt too much. I tried to listen to the voices but they faded away.

When my eyes finally opened, the voices were clear but I didn't want to get up. My head felt too heavy to lift.

"Come on, Big Guy, you can do it." *Shorty is so sweet, she always tries to make things right, but I don't think I can get up; not yet, maybe later.*

She nuzzled my neck. I could feel her breath on my broken face. It almost felt good. *Please don't touch it.*

"Big Guy, it's time to go inside and we don't want to leave you here," Yellow Dog said.

I lifted my head, which was lighter than I'd thought but it hurt more than I expected. I tried to lie back down but Shorty stood in the way.

"Don't go to sleep again," she said. "You need to get up. That other horse is gone and Jane is calling us in early. I think she knows something happened out here. Get *up*, we're waiting for you."

I was just beaten up by a horse almost as small as Brownie. Why are they hanging back for me?

"Come on, Big Guy, stretch your front legs out. I'll be here when you get up, you can lean on me." *Slippy's solid body might keep me from falling over.*

Extending my front legs made my head hurt more. If I wait too long I'll want to lie down again—*just make yourself get up, Right Now.*

Why didn't I get up?

Do it!

I was on my feet, not sure how, but my hooves were on the ground, Slippy on my left, Noble Road on my right. The two biggest horses stood with me until I took a step. Two shaky steps and I could walk. Not fast, but I could walk.

"You can all go ahead, I'll walk with Big Guy," Shorty said.

The herd spread into an awkward line meandering toward the barn. No one cantered or even trotted. They all waited for me. I was the last horse in the barn.

"Oh, Big Guy, he got you too." Jane rested her hand on my neck and walked with me to my stall. She looked at my face. "No, no, no . . ." She examined the rest of my body, discovering every wound.

Jane went straight to the phone. "Ben, you need to come down here and see what that horse did to the school horses.

"Smokey's bleeding, Brownie's limping, and I think Big Guy may have a fractured skull.

"I specifically told her NOT to put her horse in that field.

"I have to call the vet."

"Fortunately, there's more bone than brain here." The vet cradled my head in his extended forearms, examining my face.

I resented the implication that my brain was small.

"He definitely has a broken facial bone, and it's closer to his brain than I would like, but he seems to be functioning okay. The dent in his face will be permanent. I can only imagine how much this hurts. My head aches just looking at it," he said.

I have a dent in my face? I imagined the dish in Smokey's face. Arabian horses have a "dish" between their eyes and muzzle. The dish-face is considered an attractive feature. What would it look like in the middle of my forehead? It did not sound attractive.

"What can we do for it?" Jane asked.

"Not much. I could bring my mobile X-ray unit in and see exactly what's broken, but it would be an expense you don't need and it won't change his prognosis or treatment. I'll X-ray Brownie's leg to make sure it's not broken. We can't let him hobble around on a fracture.

"Big Guy's treatment will consist of cold compresses and stall-rest. There's no putting bone crushed like a soda cracker back together. Good nursing care is all you can offer."

"I gave him a bran mash," Jane said. "I thought it would be hard for him to chew grain right now."

"That's a good idea. You'll be surprised by how fast he recovers though," Dr. Loewith said. "Smokey's wound will take the longest. We need to keep him quiet. I don't want him to tug at the stitches. Keep him on a bran mash, too, until he can go outside.

"Brownie's leg is bruised, but the X-rays are clean and he's a tough little guy. I left you some Bute for his pain. You should cold hose it and give him some rest. He'll be his feisty old self in no time."

Nothing broken is good, but why did Brownie butt in like that? I'll ask him later, when we're all on the mend.

"I can't believe one horse did this much damage in less than two hours," Jane said.

"It sounds like your visitor thought he was a wild stallion fighting for position. We've all seen geldings like that," the vet said.

"Yeah, I had one," Jane said. "Jimmy was sweet as pie to ride and work with, but I couldn't let him out with another horse. We had mirrors in the indoor ring, so we could see if our horse was straight riding down the long side of the arena. I turned horses out inside when the weather was bad, but I couldn't do that with Jimmy. He would attack his own reflection in the mirror. He didn't recognize that guy and had to let him know who was boss."

"Horses evolved in the wild, and every herd needs a leader," Dr. Loewith said. "It looks like Big Guy fought for his herd. I can't believe a fifteen-hand quarter horse took on a seventeen-hand Thoroughbred. I would have bet on Big Guy."

"So would I," Jane said. "I wonder how this happened."

I wanted to defend myself, tell them I was distracted when Brownie got hurt. I could have beaten that horse. I should have won. *What is the herd going to think of me now?*

Their eyes said it all. They hadn't seen my face since the big fight.

"Does your head still hurt?" Paper Moon asked.

"That's some dent you got there," said Golden Boy. I was sure his Thoroughbred face looked gorgeous, while mine would never be the same.

"That Champ guy was bleeding all over the place when he left here." Was Slippy trying to make me feel better?

That conversation wore out and we set to grazing and wandering, the sun so bright it made my head ache. I'd been eating my hay out of a net hanging from the wall, so I didn't have to put my head down to eat. Grazing felt strange—not quite painful, but not quite right.

Is the herd avoiding me, or is it my imagination? Smokey and Brownie were still in the barn; Jane didn't think they were well enough to be outside yet. We'd been kept inside for days, trying to recover. I thought they would think less of me for losing the fight, but they didn't seem to care about that.

Jane had taken us down to the show barn during the day so we wouldn't get excited when the school horses ran out of the barn in the morning or back in at night. It's easy to get excited when everyone else is going outside and we can't. We were separated from the others for most of the day.

"I was there for you, Big Guy," Brownie announced as soon as he was in the box stall next to me.

I didn't have the heart to tell him that being distracted by him was part of the reason I got clobbered. "You shouldn't have gone after that guy," I said. "He was bigger than you."

"But I'm tough." Brownie tried to stretch his fourteen hands to an imposing height. "He was only one hand taller; four inches don't make that much difference."

"I had more than eight inches on him and look what he did to me. This is embarrassing."

"It's not your fault," Smokey said. "He was sneaky, pretending to be sorry and then launching on Shorty like that."

"Yeah, I still should have done better." I'd lost a battle with a horse not much bigger than a pony. How could I live that down?

"I think the dent in your face looks good," Brownie said.

"You look tough."

I wasn't feeling tough. I wondered what Ding and Taylor Maid would think of my face. My show horse looks were gone forever. There had been very little blood, the skin barely broken, but the bones mushed between my eyes left a crater. That's what Jane called it, a crater. I couldn't see what it looked like but I could see the faces of humans and horses when they saw it.

In our slip stalls at night, Shorty and Bucky tried to console me but that made it worse.

"He tricked you," Shorty said.

"You were trying to help Brownie when he kicked you. It wasn't your fault." Bucky shook her head for added affect.

"Yeah, yeah, he still beat me."

"You didn't see what he looked like after the fight," Shorty said. "His head was bleeding and he had cuts and scrapes all over his body."

"Just like me."

"No, much worse than you," Bucky said. "If Brownie hadn't butted in, you would have won that fight."

"Don't be so hard on Brownie, he was trying to help," I said.

"But he didn't," Shorty said. "I know he meant well, but he got in your way."

Shorty and Bucky had seen what happened. They knew

I was worried about Brownie when I got kicked. I didn't think the other horses noticed, though. *They must think I'm a big loser.*

Chapter 33

Balloons

"I think they're balloons."

I didn't know what balloons were, but I didn't like what I saw rolling along the pasture toward us.

"They're definitely balloons." Slippy was sure of himself. "I saw them a lot when I was with the circus."

"I saw them when I did pony rides at the carnival," Smokey said. "When they get loose, sometimes they float away, and sometimes they drop to the ground and slink along like armadillos."

"Didn't they have balloons at horse shows?" Slippy asked.

"I've never seen a balloon or an armadillo—whatever that is . . ." Balloons didn't look good to me. They moved with little squeaky noises and brushed along the ground. I couldn't see their feet.

"Armadillos are like little scaly pigs," Smokey said. "I saw them when the carnival traveled down South. They're scary little guys."

How do I fight a balloon? Maybe I can scare it away. I took a wide stance, ready to protect my herd from something I'd never seen before.

Weeks after the Big Fight—that's what it was known as—I still worried about what the other horses thought of me. Life was getting back to normal; Smokey and Brownie were back in the field with us and we roamed and grazed as usual.

Slippy stood slightly behind me. "Balloons are weird. They don't really talk, they just squeak and scrape. Then they shoot, like a gun. My person, years ago, used to ride me when he went hunting. Balloons make noises like gunshots, then they disappear," he said.

"Jason declared himself a great hunter every time he killed something. He'd tie the animal he'd killed behind the saddle, and I had to carry it home. I didn't like that."

"What did he do with balloons?" I watched the odd thing approaching.

"He never shot balloons, but the sound of his gun is like the noise balloons make. Balloons must not be very good shots because I've never seen them kill anything. But I would stay away from them, just in case."

Slippy is sure they're balloons, and he's afraid of them. How do I fight an animal that has no teeth or claws? "It has three heads and they're round, like human heads."

"No," Slippy said. "That's three of them together. They do that a lot. I can't believe you've never seen a balloon before."

How could heads travel by themselves? Their eyes weren't in the right place and they were looking in all directions, but they were coming straight at us.

The herd pulled away from me, and Slippy went with them. I could smell the balloons now. They smelled like the gloves the vet wore. *What is this strange animal?* It wavered, maybe it's going to go around me. I was hoping it would wander out of our field, the way it wandered in, but the wind picked up and the balloons raced toward me.

I reared up to show them how big I was. The balloons didn't care, they moved faster, lifting off the ground. Without legs they galloped toward me. I struck out and knocked them down. I heard a gunshot. *Did it get me?* I saw two heads now. *Did it shoot itself or is it behind me?*

I spun around—nothing there. I spun back, and the two heads lunged toward my back legs. I kicked. It made the same popping noise and a second head disappeared. It missed me again.

The last balloon was running away from me. Slippy and the others were cantering away, but Shorty lagged behind. The balloon aimed at her and picked up speed. I had to get that thing before it attacked Shorty.

Catching the balloon, I struck once more. The same explosive sound left me standing on its limp body. All that was left was its skin. Where had it gone? The herd stopped, taking tentative steps toward me, ears perked, ready to run if another balloon showed up. I stepped back from the skin lying on the ground.

"That's what balloons do." Slippy led the herd back up the hill. "They make all that noise and then they die, just like that."

I sniffed the carcass. Slippy did the same. "Smells terrible, doesn't it?"

"A bee stung me once and then it died," Shorty said. "Maybe they're like big bees."

"I've watched children play with balloons," Slippy said. "And when they shoot, the kids cry. Maybe they get stung."

"Kids cry when the balloons float away too," Smokey said.

"Balloons are complicated," Slippy said.

I walked down toward the stream to get away from the smell of dead balloons. My herd followed.

"That was brave of you," Shorty said, after we had been grazing for a while.

"I don't know what balloons are," I said. "They move like they're alive but when they die their skin is all that's left of them—like they weren't really there at all."

I looked back at where the balloons had died, wondering if they might wake up again.

Chapter 34

Shorty's Sick

"I don't feel so good." Shorty hadn't touched her breakfast. I'd eaten my grain before I noticed she wasn't eating. "Do you think the fresh grass was too rich? I got sick the first spring I spent in our pasture." I, like many horses, had suffered a few bouts of colic in my life.

"That's why Jane doesn't leave us outside as long when the grass first turns green," Bucky said. "I don't like going out late and coming in early, but I think that's why she does it that way. My people used to do that too." This is Bucky's second spring with us, so she now knows the program.

"I felt awful that first spring in the pasture," I said. "The vet came and put a tube in my nose—*yuk*. He pumped oil into my stomach, gave me a shot, and I felt better right away."

"Jane will take care of this," Shorty said.

She doesn't sound sick, but she didn't eat and that's not good.

"It's Monday, and the Monday-men don't notice things the way Jane does," Bucky said.

I started to worry for my friend.

"I'm used to lush, green grass in the spring," Shorty said. "This doesn't feel like that. I think it might be too many apples and carrots—too much of a good thing."

"You did have a lot of students bring you treats over the weekend." I try not to be jealous when Shorty gets so much attention. I should be a bigger horse than that.

Bucky was right, the Monday-men didn't notice that Shorty hadn't eaten her breakfast, and they had us out in the pasture early. We grazed but Shorty stood under a tree, her head drooped. She walked around a little and tried to eat, but I don't think she swallowed a mouthful all morning. By midday she felt so bad, she lay on the ground rolling around, trying to relieve the pain.

"Shorty, don't do that. I knew a horse who twisted an intestine while doing that." I didn't want to tell her how that had ended.

"I just hurt." She rolled over again.

I watched her legs in the air and wondered how many apples she'd been fed yesterday. If she weren't so popular she wouldn't be sick. *Her popularity might kill her*, I thought.

Clink, the latch banged against the metal gate and Jane was running toward us. How did she know Shorty was sick? She's wearing a dress—I've never seen Jane in a dress, but the black rubber boots are familiar.

"Shorty, come on girl, get up." Jane led Shorty toward the barn. "It's a good thing I looked out the window while I was getting ready to go have lunch with my mom. You poor thing, you're soaking wet."

"Jane will take care of her now," Slippy said.

I watched them walk toward the barn, thinking of the many times I'd seen a case of colic go horribly wrong. I was a foal when I first heard a colic being treated, in the aisle in front of my stall. I remember pieces of the vet's comments: ". . . colic . . . catchall term for any digestive upset . . . impaction . . . twisted gut . . . surgery . . . don't let him roll, keep him walking . . . the most common cause of death in horses . . ."

I'd stood a little closer to my mother that day.

The lush grass around me turned sour, like my mood. I nibbled and looked at the barn, and nibbled again and wondered what was happening in there. I discovered Brownie grazing next to me.

I remembered back to weaning day, when we were all about six months old and left in the pasture without our mothers. We were frantic, running in circles, calling out for the mares. I'd wondered where my mother was and when she would be back. I didn't know I would never see her again. Brownie grazed near us as if nothing was wrong. After a while, the foals and I did the same. We'd followed him wherever he went, the way we had followed our mothers.

I looked at the barn again, hoping to see Shorty, and I was glad Brownie was close by. Losing Shorty would feel like losing my mother all over again. Brownie wasn't moving around much today, but I would follow him like a baby if he did.

The chain was up behind Shorty's stall when we came into the barn, but her stall was empty. Eating my afternoon grain was a chore.

Jane had changed from her dress into blue jeans, and stood in the aisle to announce: "Shorty's in the indoor arena, the vet has treated her, and the meds for pain are working."

"You know they can't understand you." The Monday-man stood next to her with his thumbs hooked on his bib overalls, laughing.

"I know," she said. "But I feel better telling them."

The Monday-man shuffled toward the show barn, still chuckling.

"It doesn't look good, gang." Jane was almost whispering. "It doesn't look good at all."

I had known four horses who didn't recover from colic,

but I had known a lot more who'd pulled through. I didn't ask the others what they were thinking; we didn't talk. I lay on the floor with Lady Bug curled up near my chest, but we didn't sleep. I wondered if anyone slept. Lady Bug's purring was usually soothing, but not this night.

Our herd would be so different without Shorty. She'd reminded me of my mother from the start. I kept thinking about Jane's words, "it doesn't look good." *Come on, Shorty, pull through this. I don't know what I'd do without you.*

We could hear Jane making noise near the door to the arena.

"She's making herself a bed out of hay bales so she can keep an eye on Shorty all night." Brownie could see what she was doing from his stall.

The grain wheelbarrow appeared in the morning at the usual hour, so I guess I'd dozed off. Jane was half-asleep but kept our morning on schedule.

"Shorty's out of the woods, gang. She's eating hay and passing oily manure."

I wondered if the other horses were as relieved as I was. Shorty, sweet Shorty, was okay!

Did Jane put something extra in the grain today? It's especially tasty.

Chapter 35

A Real Horse

Fear of losing Shorty made me look at life differently. I was proud to be a school horse. I used to think my life was perfect as a show horse. I'd had a big box stall to myself, I was groomed until my coat shone, and praised by Nancy and the people around me.

But between shows, back on the farm, show horses were in their stalls about twenty hours a day. We were turned out for an hour or two, and exercised for the same length of time most days. I loved that life, but it seemed boring now. Except for the horse shows—I still missed them.

I thought about my friend Kaiser and wondered how he was doing. He was foaled out in the open, on a Montana ranch. He didn't talk about it much, but he hadn't made the cut as a ranch horse. Shorty told me that Kaiser had been afraid of the cattle. Maybe that's why he didn't talk about it. Now he was living with a pony. I wondered if he pushed her around, or if he had softened up by now.

I thought about all the school horses.

Nugget was a western pleasure horse in his show days.

Star Shadow had been a backyard horse, belonging to a family with three girls and three horses, but she'd adjusted to being a school horse when the girls grew up and moved away.

Noble Road had been a fox hunter. He got to gallop cross-country, jumping fences. But Noble's owner got old and stopped riding, and when his family took over the farm, Noble became a school horse. When Ben picked him up, the people who'd inherited the farm didn't even know their father's favorite horse's name. That's how he became Noble Road; it was on the street sign at the corner.

I thought about Slippy's life in the circus and Smokey's rodeo days.

Golden Boy occasionally bragged about his racing years.

Paper Moon never shared her story, so I could imagine something amazing for her—maybe she carried royalty in parades.

When I joined the school string, I'd thought my story was special—I'd been a top show horse. But all of us were something else before we became school horses. Except Shorty—she had always been a school horse. She said she loved feeling young riders develop enough confidence to canter and jump over fences.

If I'd kept showing, I never would've learned how great it was to be in a herd. Kaiser used to say, "We're herd animals, it's our nature."

I thought of how I'd felt back then—groomed to perfection, jumping big fences—and how I feel today, shaggy and warm. Now, I'm standing in a pasture with horses I used to feel sorry for—and I love it. I have hair sticking out of my ears, my whiskers are long, and my winter coat is thick. I used to think the school horses looked shabby, but now I see them as snug and comfortable—and I am one of them.

I could almost hear Kaiser's voice in the rustle of falling leaves: "Now you're a real horse."

No, Kaiser, I've always been a real horse. We're all real horses.

Glossary

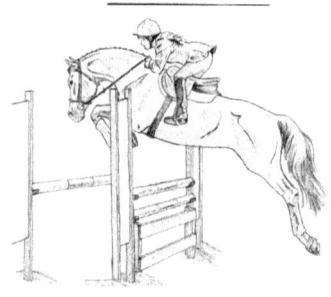

Bit – The part of the bridle that fits in a horse's mouth and helps in the communication between the horse and rider.

Bridle – A bridle is a piece of leather headgear that holds the bit and reins.

Canter – A three beat gait between the trot and gallop.

Colic – A term for a digestive upset in horses. It can vary greatly in severity; from a little gas to a bowel blockage or twisted intestine.

Colt – A male foal under the age of two.

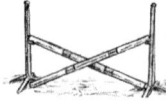 **Cross-pole** – A low jump consisting of crossed poles; usually used as a warm up jump.

Equitation – The art and practice of horsemanship.

Equitation class – A division at a horse show in which the rider's performance is being judged, not the horse.

Filly – A female foal under the age of two.

Foal – A young horse, male or female, under the age of two.

Gait – The manner or pace of movement.

Gallop – A three beat gait faster than the canter. When a horse runs full out he is galloping.

Hand - Means by which a horse's height is determined. A hand is four inches. A horse that measures 14.3 is fourteen hands three inches tall, at the highest point of the withers.

Hydrotherapy – Using water to treat injuries or soothe tired legs at the end of a hard workout.

Lead – When horses canter or gallop one front leg extends more than the other. Turning to the left, the left front extends more; to the right, the right front extends more. Horses naturally change lead when they change direction.

Lead change – When a horse, moving in a canter or gallop, changes from one lead to the other.

Oxer – A jump using more than one set of standards, giving the fence width and height.

Polo wrap – An elastic bandage often used on wounds or as leg protection during exercise.

Saddle skirt – A part of the saddle that extends, or hangs down, from the saddle. The upper portion of the rider's leg rests against the skirt.

School horse – A horse used to give riding lessons.

Scoliosis – A lateral curvature of the spine; different from the body's natural front to back curve.

Snaffle bit – A mild bit, joint in the center, easy on the horse's mouth.

Slip stall (also called a **standing stall**) – A

stall that is wide enough for the horse to stand up and lay down but does not allow room for the horse to turn around in.

Trot – The gait between walk and canter. The horse lifts each diagonal pair of legs together.

Vertical – A simple fence without depth. (see image above)

Withers – Part of the horse's spine that projects upwards between the shoulder blades, at the base of the neck. It's the point at which a horse's height is measured.

Author's Note

The horses in this book are real. I worked with them for years and got to know their kind spirits, talents and personalities. I am glad to have the opportunity to share these characters with you. The image below depicts me changing a light bulb while standing on Slippy's back. He was so calm, and his back was broad enough to use as a table, which he allowed me to do many times, although I did not do this alone; someone was holding his lead rope and handing me light bulbs.

Most of these horses stayed with me into their old age. I thought you might want to know that Kaiser did fully recover and lived a long peaceful life. I figured out how to keep Bucky from opening gates: by putting the latch low enough so she couldn't reach it.

Acknowledgments

There are many humans to acknowledge for their assistance in bringing this book to print. My early readers Lisa Caloia and Fay Kozlowski kept me on track. There are many who did not know that my comments and questions had to do with a book in progress. Thank you, dear friends, for being there to listen and adding valuable insights.

Rootstock Publishing has assisted me again and I thank them for their expertise and patience with an unschooled author. My goal from the start was to produce a quality book and Rootstock did not disappoint. Samantha Kolber was with me from start to finish. Eddie Vincent's cover and interior design work are great, as always. Rootstock put it all together for me again with *Big Guy*. To the behind the scenes staff that I have not had the opportunity to meet: Thank you one and all.

Kathy Connell's illustrations exceeded my expectations, and I expected a lot. Thank you for the time, effort, and acceptance of changes and additions. Your work shines.

Joni Cole and the White River Junction Writer's Group are worth their weight in gold. Joni's guidance and spirit keep our sessions on track. Each writer who shared and commented is part of this book. Thanks to each and every one of you.

My dear friend Lois Robbins was one of my early readers for my first three books. She was unable to read *Big Guy*, due to illness and failing eyesight, but I was able to share my manuscript with her and her assistance, as always, was priceless. I will miss you forever Lois.

My husband, Don, is always last on this list but first in every other way.

About the Author

Celia's first career was with horses. She trained horses and taught students on Southeast Michigan's hunter jumper circuit for more than thirty years. The characters in this book, horse and human, are based on people and animals she has known.

Her second career sent her back to school to study gardening fine arts and landscape design. They were not just careers, they were passions and when life left room for a new passion she began to distance hike. Celia has kept journals and written short stories and poems all of her life. She has attended classes at local universities and writing seminars and has written articles for newsletters, local newspapers, and The Vermont League of Writers; she has been working on her craft for decades.

Celia Ryker's first book, *Walking Home: Trail Stories*, was a Gold Winner in the 2022 Human Relations Indie Book Award in Travel, and Silver Winner in Motivational Memoir and Personal Determination. Her second book, *Augusta: A Novel*, about her grandmother's life of hardship at the turn of the twentieth century, won the 2023 Literary Titan Gold Book Award.

About the Artist

Dr. Kathy Connell was raised in Northern Illinois, and has had horses in her life since she was a child. Her love of horses led her to become an equine veterinarian. After completing veterinary school in Illinois, and an internship in Florida, Kathy moved to Michigan where she worked for fifteen years with the author's husband, Don. Kathy then moved to Oregon where she continues to work as an equine veterinarian. As an artist, Kathy draws, paints, and sculpts. She's recently begun carving and building wooden rocking horses. She enjoys woodworking, improving her home with her husband, wild truffle hunting with her Labrador retrievers, and agility training with her Icelandic sheepdog, Loki.

More Children's Titles from Rootstock Publishing:

Lucy Dancer by Eva Zimet

No Excuses by Stephen. L. Harris

Pauli Murray's Revolutionary Life by Simki Kuznick

Street of Storytellers by Doug Wilhelm

The Violin Family by Melissa Perley

Rootstock Publishing is a curated hybrid and traditional publishing house collaborating with authors—the rootstock of creative content. Rootstock's books have won multiple awards, including, among others, the Eric Hoffer Award, the IPPY, Foreword INDIES, the IBPA Ben Franklin Award, Literary Titan, and IPNE Award. Founded in 2017 in Montpelier, Vermont, Rootstock has published more than sixty books of fiction, nonfiction, poetry, and children's books by authors from all over the globe.

To learn more visit www.rootstockpublishing.com.

Printed in the USA
CPSIA information can be obtained
at www.ICGtesting.com
LVHW011115280624
784121LV00009BA/114